D0414180

Major Harold Ferguson: Citizen-Soldier Meets Roaring 20s Los Angeles

Major Harold Ferguson: Citizen-Soldier Meets Roaring 20s Los Angeles

Edmond J. Clinton III

Copyright © 2019 by Edmond J. Clinton III.

Library of Congress Control Number: 2018914565
ISBN: Hardcover   978-1-9845-7139-7
               Softcover   978-1-9845-7138-0
               eBook   978-1-9845-7137-3

All rights reserved. No part of this book may be reproduced or transmitted in any form or by any means, electronic or mechanical, including photocopying, recording, or by any information storage and retrieval system, without permission in writing from the copyright owner.

The views expressed in this work are solely those of the author and do not necessarily reflect the views of the publisher, and the publisher hereby disclaims any responsibility for them.

Certain stock imagery © Getty Images.

Print information available on the last page.

Rev. date: 12/17/2018

To order additional copies of this book, contact:
Xlibris
1-888-795-4274
www.Xlibris.com
Orders@Xlibris.com
781670

This book is dedicated to Harold Ferguson's two nieces, Eleanor Gleason Grossman and Lillian Gleason Garrison who still have fond memories of their uncle.

MAP OF CAPTAIN FERGUSON'S 143RD FIELD ARTILLERY TROOP MOVEMENT

FRANCE, August 15, 1918 to September 25, 1918

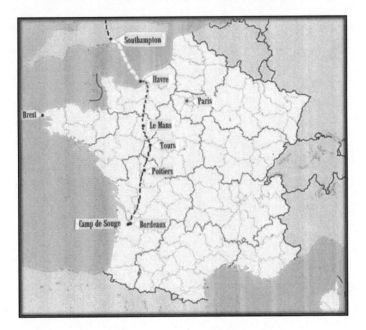

August 15, 1918: Left New York on "SS Armagh"
August 28, 1918: Went ashore at Liverpool, England to Knotty Ash US Rest Camp
August 30, 1918: Liverpool by train to Southampton, England
August 31, 1918: Southampton to Havre, France by ship "Charles"
September 2, 1918: Train leaves Havre to Le Mans
September 3, 1918: Train leaves Le Mans to Tours
September 3, 1918: Train leaves Tours for Poitiers at French army barracks
September 16, 1918: Train leaves Poitiers for Cadaujac via Bordeaux
September 25, 1918: Regiment marched to Camp de Souge (20 miles)

Contents

Preface ix

Introduction xiii

Chapter 1   Harold Ferguson Signs Up 1

Chapter 2   America Enters World War I 7

Chapter 3   Captain Ferguson Arrives in France 21

Chapter 4   Influenza Pandemic of 1917–19 29

Chapter 5   The Armistice and Food Relief 53

Chapter 6   Harold Ferguson Comes Home 73

Chapter 7   The American Legion 83

Chapter 8   Organized Labor in Southern California 93

Chapter 9   The Red Scare 111

Chapter 10 Hollywood and Lankershim Ranch 129

Chapter 11 Angel City Boom of the 1920s 139

Chapter 12 Harold G. Ferguson Corporation, 1924–31 159

Chapter 13 Stock Market Crash and San Quentin 179

Chapter 14 Post–World War I and the Great Depression 197

Conclusion 221

Bibliography 225

Index 233

Preface

Until recently, my in-laws rarely talked about "Uncle Harold Ferguson," who served as a soldier in World War I, was a major player in the exploding real estate market of 1920s Los Angeles and was sentenced to jail in 1931 for grand larceny and securities violations. These events occurred in the lead-up to the Great Depression. When a box of Harold's personal papers, photographs, and diary were discovered, details of his life were uncovered. After researching a biography of my grandfather, Clifford Clinton, and his cafeteria in 1930s Los Angeles (*Clifton's and Clifford Clinton: A Cafeteria and a Crusader,* Angel City Press, 2015), I had developed an interest in this period. Ferguson was a significant part of the development of Los Angeles, and the challenge was to juxtapose his life and work in real estate with the events of the 1920s. He had an impact on Los Angeles, but Los Angeles confronted him in ways he hadn't expected.

This man's family name was already familiar to me since my maternal grandfather, Vernon Ferguson, had developed quite a reputation in the lore of the city both as an assistant district attorney in the 1930s under District Attorney Buron Fitts and as a defense attorney, in the last years of his life, for Mickey Cohen. As far as I know, there is no direct family connection between the two Fergusons, but I was accustomed to hearing family stories of the Los Angeles Fergusons.

I wish to thank many who have helped with the research and writing of this narrative. My wife Diane has been an indefatigable editor and researcher. She exceeded my expectations when she translated Harold's chicken scratches and partial diary entries into a readable manuscript that allowed analysis of his World War I experience by a distant generation.

In reading and critiquing my exploratory manuscript, Merry Ovnick of the *Southern California Quarterly* provided valuable ideas and understanding of the period, making it possible for me to expand an initial manuscript into this book. Paul Wormser, director of the Sherman Library and Gardens, was most helpful and generous with his assistance, making available to us scrapbooks gifted to the library decades ago by Harold's sister Dorothy Ferguson. These books contain much of the original newspaper material of the time and helped to fill in gaps in the narrative. The Los Angeles Central Library provided microfiche records of newspaper reports during Harold's active years, and the Newport Beach Public Library provided access to the *Los Angeles Times* reporting during Ferguson's trial.

For an understanding of the history of Los Angeles in this period, I had a head start. Having grown up in the Los Feliz neighborhood in the 1940s and '50s, I have vivid memories of the landscapes, geography, businesses, and entertainment venues of Hollywood and downtown Los Angeles. My aunt Jean Clinton Roeschlaub helped me write job descriptions for Clifton's Cafeteria employees and invited me to the Hollywood Bowl to experience this open-air music venue. My younger brother and I attended music concerts at the Greek Theatre. When I worked as a busboy at my grandfather's cafeteria, Clifton's, on Seventh and Broadway Streets in downtown during summer vacations, the life of the inner city came alive.

Eleanor Gleason Grossman and Lillian Gleason Garrison, Harold's nieces, have provided important memories of the man they knew and loved. They remember a selfless individual who had personal qualities of intelligence and strong character and who weathered the storms of the 1930s with fortitude, never losing his self-respect and family ties.

Clay Stalls of the Huntington Library gave me direction in researching the food-relief program of World War I. Olga Tsapina, also of Huntington, helped to organize and catalog Harold's private papers, photos, and diary in preparation for their place in a permanent collection.

Last, my course of study at Occidental College in 1964–65, a two-year program on the "History of Civilization," taught me to see historical periods through the lens of many disparate but interconnected events and individuals.

Introduction

When Harold Gale Ferguson was a child, his family left Canada to establish new roots in Los Angeles. His formative years were idyllic, and he became a Stanford-educated lawyer, but storm clouds from a global conflict derailed his aspirations when he and two million others were sent to Europe in 1917 to fight the "war to end all wars." This dramatic turn of events not only altered his career plans; it also opened up his city to the problems of Europe and the world. As a member of the National Guard, thirty-year-old Ferguson was sent to France as a captain during the final months of World War I. Upon his return as Major Ferguson, he began life anew in "Roaring Twenties" Los Angeles—an unstable and chaotic environment marked by a population explosion and a "get rich quick" mentality. What Major Ferguson and millions of others couldn't forsee was that the beneficial effects provided by the American government and farmers to World War I European food relief would play a role in the development of the Great Depression.

For decades prior to the start of World War I in 1914 and US involvement in 1917, a majority of the general public had strongly opposed any involvement in European conflicts. This deeply held belief in the need for isolation from European affairs and entanglements would persist into the postwar period, as many remained convinced that our participation in the war had had far-reaching negative economic and social consequences. Although some militarists such as former president Theodore Roosevelt and citizens of French and German extraction favored early intervention, President Woodrow Wilson kept his own counsel and deferred the decision to intervene. When Wilson eventually declared war on Germany, the US Army, under the guidance of the president, formed the American

Expeditionary Force (AEF) led by General John ("Black Jack") Pershing.

Thus, citizen-soldiers were suddenly sent to fight "against the Hun" and to give their all for a country across the Atlantic Ocean that was in dire need of their help. Because the standing US Army was insufficient to support such an immense engagement, many of the young men and women came from the National Guard, voluntary enlistments, and the draft. What emerged was a fighting force with little experience and training in trench warfare, a limited supply of weapons, and few troop carriers to ferry them across the Atlantic. But with their spirit of patriotism, youthful exuberance, and moral outrage, they managed to turn the tide against the Central Powers. The Americans brought new hope to depleted, demoralized European Allies helping to end the conflict. This was not victory; it was cessation of war—an armistice.

Libraries are full of World War I histories, photographs, and newsreels, as well as recent books aimed at familiarizing succeeding generations with this seminal conflict as the centennial of the armistice approaches. They give readers valuable insight into the military, political, and economic aspects of the conflagration of 1914—detailing battles, alliances, and the geography of the war. Acres of cemeteries with both marked and unmarked graves silently testify to individuals' final sacrifices for their countries. Twenty-first-century readers still find it hard to grasp the carnage, futility, destruction, and indifference to human life of this war of attrition.

Some elements of the conflict remain in the background in publications that have mainly focused on combat, including (1) the global influenza pandemic that collided with the events of the conflict and (2) the roles played by Herbert Hoover,

Woodrow Wilson, and the US government in food relief, saving millions of famine victims, including children in Europe and postwar Russia. These subjects and more were addressed in the diary of Harold Gale Ferguson, an AEF soldier who had firsthand experience with both elements. Discovering our great-uncle's diary gave us a firsthand account of these events.

While researching this period, I learned of Hoover's and Wilson's role in a massive American humanitarian food-rescue operation during and following the Great War. This relief effort, begun in 1914 and ending in 1924, saved millions of citizens, from both Allied and combatant nations, from starvation and disease. This reminded me of my recent biography of my grandfather, Clifford Clinton, founder of Los Angeles–based Clifton's Cafeteria in 1931, who undertook food relief to Europe after World War II to reduce famine among civilian adults and children. His foundation, Meals for Millions, shipped tons of dry-food supplements to countries in Europe and locations in America. Learning of such crusades by dedicated individuals and groups became an optimistic counterpoint to reading of the inhumane destructive forces of war.

As the armistice went into effect, survivors of the Great War (1914–18) were ready to come home and restart their lives, leaving the killing fields of France behind. For many, Los Angeles was home, and they wanted to resume a peaceful life with a new optimism to replace the terrible fear, unpredictability, and chaos of war—to reconnect with parents, wives, and children.

In describing the postwar era in Los Angeles in his review of Robert Gottlieb and Irene Wolt's *Thinking Big: The Story of the Los Angeles Times*, Carey McWilliams says that "it [the history of the *Times*] is more than the story of the *Times*: it is really a large part of the story of Los Angeles. It is, also, very much a part of a larger story—the dynamics of expansionism, of free enterprise run amuck."[1]

This is a case history of the culture of 1920s Los Angeles and its impact on veteran Harold Ferguson, whose solid character and trustworthy demeanor propelled him to achieve great success in one of the most dynamic growth industries in the city's history—real estate. But he couldn't outlast the downturn of 1929, which destroyed his business and his livelihood.

---

[1]   R. Gottlieb and Irene Wolt, *Thinking Big: The Story of the Los Angeles Times, Its Publishers, and Their Influence on Southern California* (New York: G. P. Putnam's Sons, 1977).

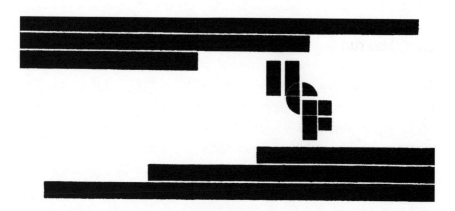

Chapter 1

Harold Ferguson Signs Up

As we approach the one hundredth anniversary of the armistice ending World War I (the eleventh hour of the eleventh day of the eleventh month of 1918), much of this conflict has faded into the mists of history, replaced by the memories of more recent wars, including World War II, Korea, Vietnam, and the current violent global insurgency of radical Islamists.

Our family's discovery of a handwritten "A Line a Day" diary buried in a box in a closet gave us a very personal account of an American soldier's experience as part of the American Expeditionary Force in France and Italy during the last months of the war. Harold Ferguson, a great-uncle, saw the Spanish flu, which killed millions, including fellow soldiers. Never directly involved in combat, Major Ferguson became a manager in one of the largest food-relief programs in history during his stint in Trieste, Italy. Under the guidance of Herbert Hoover, the American Relief Administration distributed mostly American food products to desperately undernourished individuals throughout all of war-torn Europe and Russia.

Born in Vancouver, British Columbia, Canada, on August 31, 1888, Harold Gale Ferguson moved with his family to California when he was six months old. The family settled in Riverside. When he was five, his parents, Peter and Lillian Prest Ferguson, moved with their children—Harold, Dorothy, and Warren—to 6937 Prospect Avenue in Hollywood. In 1912, his family moved again to Hollywood Boulevard and Orange Avenue, where the present-day Grauman's Chinese Theatre is located. Harold grew up in a strict Scottish Presbyterian home environment and had his heart set on becoming a doctor. After graduating from Hollywood High School, he entered Stanford University (known as "The Farm") in the fall of 1907 as a premed student. But after a few months, family pressure made him change his major to prelaw; many of his relatives were attorneys.

His family provided him with a small stipend to attend college, which he supplemented with part-time work picking melons for $2.50 per day in the Imperial Valley during the summer. He also pitched hay and loaded hay bales into burning-hot boxcars in the San Joaquin Valley.

He joined the Delta Kappa Epsilon fraternity and was active in track and field at Stanford. His college career was highly successful and colorful. He worked on the *Daily Palo Alto*, which became the *Stanford Daily*, and worked his way up to editor during his senior year. He was elected to the Press Club (an organization of Stanford journalists), Phi Delta Phi (a legal fraternity), and the Quadrangle Club (an exclusive honor society), and he became president of his senior class and his fraternity. He was actively involved in student affairs. He graduated prelaw in 1911.

He took and passed the California bar examination and entered private law practice in the Douglas Building at Third and

Spring Streets in downtown Los Angeles. His first months of practice were a disappointment since he was both bored and not making any income, although he was able to survive on private property management from his father's estate. He had some funds to buy a ranch in Lankershim, which he managed. He then became aware of and applied for an opening in the Los Angeles city prosecutor's office. He had to pass a civil service examination first, so he spent his evenings and free time studying for it. He eventually passed and was hired as deputy city prosecutor under city prosecutor Ray Nimmo at $150 per month.

He joined the California National Guard at the suggestion of several of his friends who were members. Assigned to a field artillery regiment, he applied himself to his military duties and quickly rose from private to first lieutenant. He was assigned to Battery A of the First Regiment of the California Field Artillery (FA).

In 1915, he met and married Miss Dolores Gordon (affectionately referred to as "Dot" in his diary). The wedding was performed in Riverside.

After many months as a deputy prosecutor, he left his job with the city of Los Angeles to set up a private law practice. Global events changed his future, however. In June 1916, his National Guard unit was ordered to New Mexico to deal with a Mexican uprising.

Pancho Villa had crossed the US border and occupied Columbus, New Mexico, murdering several American citizens. This had led President Woodrow Wilson to send in the National Guard. The troops chased Villa back into Mexico, but this did not end the Mexican threat, so additional units were transferred to the area. Lieutenant Ferguson's National Guard battery was sent to Nogales, where he spent several months in military training, including long marches through the mountains to prepare for further fighting, which never materialized.

The significance of Mexico's border incursions to the entry of the US into the war was soon to become apparent. While no evidence exists to suggest Germany prompted Mexico to cross the American border, the mere fact of this incursion provided Germany with a potential alley against the United States. The Zimmermann Telegram, decrypted by British intelligence and forwarded to Washington, DC, had been sent from the German foreign minister, Arthur Zimmermann, to the German ambassador to Mexico, Heinrich von Eckhardt. It offered US territory to Mexico if Mexico would join the German cause. This message provided the final justification to the United States to end its isolationism and declare war on Germany and its allies (the Central Powers) on April 6, 1917.

Meanwhile, Ferguson's regiment had returned to Los Angeles in December 1916, and he had been mustered out in January 1917. He had returned to private law practice in the Bartlett Building at Seventh and Spring Streets in downtown Los Angeles. There, he assisted in the revision of various municipal ordinances under the city prosecutor, Irwin Widney. Little did he know that the European war was about to change his plans again.

The wartime developments necessitated that he reenlists to answer his country's call. Since he had surrendered his National Guard commission, he enlisted as a private in the 143rd Field Artillery Regiment of the California National Guard. His new unit was stationed at the Presidio. The 143rd remained in San Francisco for several months while engaged in training student officers in the First and Second Student Officers Training Camp. In early 1918, the regiment was ordered to Camp Kearney in San Diego. Shortly after this move, the

young Ferguson was quickly promoted from private to captain, becoming the adjutant officer to his regiment. In August 1918, the 143rd (Fortieth Division, 143rd FA, Battery A) was ordered to Hoboken Dock in New York, where they boarded a troop transport vessel to France as part of the AEF.

In the period that followed, Harold Ferguson candidly described his contacts, activities, and thoughts in his diary, providing a window into the life of an American officer during his ten months of duty in Europe. His diary also depicts how he adapted to life after the military, when he returned to Los Angeles in June 1919. Limited diary space necessitated abbreviated and shorthand descriptions of these events, which in this book will be expanded by annotations and historic additions.

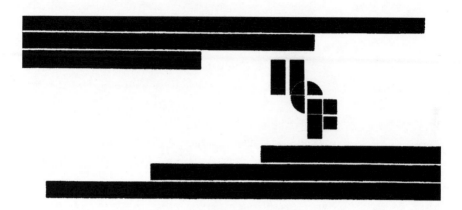

Chapter 2

America Enters World War I

America was slow to enter the war. For decades, America had held a strictly isolationist stance toward European conflicts and entanglements. The Spanish-American War in 1898 had awakened the military spirit of the country. But Europe was not Cuba, and the United States was founded on geographic and political separation from Britain and the continent. This attitude became more prevalent among the American public once it became clear how vicious and destructive this war had become. Millions of young men were being slaughtered, and there seemed to be no end to fighting.

> Since the guns had first sounded in Europe in August 1914, Americans had profoundly disagreed about the conflict and about America's relation to it. Moreover, United States in 1917 stood at the end of two decades of extraordinarily divisive political and social upheaval. Deep social fissures had been opened by the enormous concentration of private capital and economic power in "trusts," by the effort of progressive

reformers to bring the corporations under public control, by labor disturbances, and by the arrival in America of over 12 million immigrants since the turn of the century.[2]

In the early years of the war, a minority of voices advocated preparedness, however. With support from a newly founded American Legion in 1915, a group lobbied the US government to strengthen its military, staged a preparedness parade in New York City, and produced a film titled *America Prepare.* Some American businesses, aware of the fortunes to be made through manufacturing of war materiel, supported earlier entry into the war, as did some French and English Americans, whose connection with Europe was strong, and Theodore Roosevelt, known for his militarism. But Woodrow Wilson would wait. Even the U-boat sinking of the *Lusitania* in 1915 wasn't enough to bring America into the fighting.

Finally, a combination of factors broke this isolationism: urgent requests by allies Britain and France, whose fighting forces and morale were becoming depleted; the resurgence of U-boat attacks in the Atlantic to sink British warships and US ships; and the Zimmermann Telegram, which threatened to bring Mexico into the war. Americans were still divided in their support for the war, but Wilson was determined to put a positive spin on the country's chance to save Europe. So, the AEF was born, Liberty bonds were sold to the American public, and hard work began to enlist and train an effective army and transport it to France.

---

[2]   David M. Kennedy, *Over Here: The First World War and American Society* (New York: Oxford University Press, 1980), 11.

George Creel and the Committee for Public Information

The declaration of war on Germany and subsequent massive engagement of American troops in France didn't end the divisiveness and disagreement among the public about America's involvement. In April 1917, the secretaries of war, navy, and state counseled President Wilson to form a national information committee to inform and consolidate Americans' attitudes toward the war. What became the Committee for Public Information had a particularly challenging task since millions of immigrants from central, eastern, and southern Europe had recently arrived in the US, and many spoke little to no English.

Wilson chose George Creel, a muckraking journalist from the Progressive Era, to run a propaganda campaign throughout the remainder of the war. Creel's primary target was the newly arrived immigrant population who he felt deserved education and information rather than censorship and coercion—a more democratic way of convincing these Americans to support the war efforts. The Committee for Public Information placed advertisements in magazines (e.g., the *Saturday Evening Post*), organized pageants, and distributed simple foreign-language pamphlets, all designed to educate and formulate positive attitudes to support the fighting men. "Four-minute men" were trained to visit movie theaters across the country to give propaganda speeches supporting American involvement in the war during the changing of film reels. The goal was to create in the American public a uniform stance of support for the fighting men of the AEF.

America Gears Up for War

The US Army at the time of war declaration was quite small (fewer than 130,000 men), certainly unprepared to battle the

millions of fighting men who were engaged in Europe. Raising and training a large fighting force that then would have to be transferred en masse across the Atlantic would be a daunting task. "There were not enough machine guns, not enough artillery pieces, not enough uniforms, not enough ships to transport an army to Europe."[3]

The first to be chosen were National Guard units that already had military training and unit cohesion. Initially, sixteen National Guard divisions (divisions 26 through 42) were designated to go to Europe, although transportation for this many troops would require troop transport ships, which were not yet available; each American division was made up of 28,000 soldiers. This number was clearly insufficient, however, so President Wilson decided to institute the Selective Service System (a successor to the draft used in the Civil War). Relying on enlistments might have been preferable, but Wilson wanted to head off a plan by Theodore Roosevelt to lead a division of volunteers to France and thus undercut the government's authority and planning strategy.[4] Also, a draft would draw a fairer group of individuals instead of relying on certain geographic or employment sectors.

Enlistments, however, would supplement the needed troops, and young men across the country were lining up at recruiting offices to join. Some felt a sense of patriotism toward the USA, others a duty to save France; still others wanted to kill the hated Kaiser, and others went because it was expected.

---

[3]   James H. Hallas Editor, *Doughboy War, The American Expeditionary Force in WWI (Mechanicsburg, Pennsylvania, Stackpole Military History Series, 2009)*, 2.

[4]   David Stevenson, *With Our Backs to the Wall: Victory and Defeat in 1918* (London England: Penguin Books, 2011), 43.

A latter-day historian referred to them [new enlistees] as "fierce lambs." Fierce they certainly were; their combat record brooked no dispute. And yes, they were lambs, their lack of sophistication and worldliness sometimes humorous, often touching, and sometimes sad and a bit pathetic. They were farmers and mill workers, students and clerks, men whose roots went back to the original 13 colonies and men who were barely off the boat from Europe and had yet to master the English language. Few in the ranks were well educated, a surprising number (by today's standards at least) were illiterate.[5]

All new recruits were required to undergo physical examinations to ensure their fitness for duty in Europe. The worst part of the evaluation was a battery of inoculations designed to keep the troops free of infectious disease. In 1917 there was no vaccine for influenza yet since medical science had not yet identified viruses in general or this particular virus, but vaccines were given for typhoid, paratyphoid, smallpox, and typhus. During the influenza pandemic, the army also gave out over 1.5 million pneumococcus lipo vaccines. The anti-typhus vaccine was the most toxic and made most soldiers ill.[6]

General John J. Pershing was chosen to be the commander-in-chief of the AEF. He was Wilson's ideal candidate to lead US forces in France. Born in 1860 in Missouri, he had graduated from West Point and as a first lieutenant had led African American soldiers of the Tenth Cavalry against the Sioux and Apache. In 1898, he had led a regiment to Cuba to fight

---

[5]   Hallas, Doughboy War, The American Expeditionary Force in WWI, 2.

[6]   Richard S. Faulkner, *Pershing's Crusaders: The American Soldier in World War I (Lawrence, Kansas, University Press of Kansas, 2017)*, 57.

side by side with Theodore Roosevelt in the Second Cavalry Brigade. After service in the Philippines and Japan, he had been promoted directly from captain to brigadier general by Roosevelt, a testament to his leadership ability and coolness under fire. In 1916, he had commanded troops who chased Pancho Villa into Mexico after this fateful border uprising. He knew France through his travels and spoke the language.[7]

The British and French armies were desperate for additional fighting men and were hopeful that the Americans would combine with their forces to reverse their dwindling military might. General Pershing, on the other hand, was wary of "amalgamation," where his forces would come under the control of British and French armies and commanders. Although this difference regarding how the armies would collaborate would cause some tension among Allied forces, the disagreements would eventually be resolved through compromises.[8]

"Two out of three American soldiers who reached France took part in battle. A total, 2,084,000 US soldiers reached France before wars end. Of these, 1,390,000 saw active service in the front lines. 42 American divisions reached France before wars end. Of these 29 took part in active combat service. The rest were used for replacements or arrived at the hostilities ended."[9]

Although the speed of transport of the American soldiers to Europe left the Allies—particularly Prime Minister David Lloyd George of Great Britain—distressed, many of the transport obstacles were eventually resolved, and by November 1917 the AEF in France numbered over two million. Fear of expanded AEF involvement in the conflict rushed the German forces,

---

[7]   Stevenson, *With Our Backs to the Wall,* 44,249.

[8]   Stevenson, *With Our Backs to the Wall,* 43-44,250.

[9]   Faulkner, *Pershing's Crusaders,* 2.

leading them to commence offensives earlier than planned to avoid dealing with the anticipated involvement of the Americans. This precipitate action had a significant impact on the Germans' battle effectiveness, which helped turn the tide in favor of the Allies. In spring of 1918, Peyton C. March took over the duties of Chief of the General Staff and increased the transport of troops to France under the philosophy of "as soon as possible." Troopship capacity rose by 40 percent, and turnaround times for troopship trips fell to forty days by February 1918.

Training these young men to fight required a plan and organization. Much of the training was performed in military camps in the Midwest and East Coast. The earliest units, including the First Division (the Big Red One), were trained in France with the help of French soldiers, who could educate the Americans on the use of artillery, machine guns, bayonets, and grenades. The French could also instruct US soldiers on the digging of trenches and other battlefield techniques.[10]

By the time the AEF entered the war, the combatants were in a stalemate. For more than three years, the Central Powers in the eastern and western fronts and Turkey had fought the Allies in a war involving tanks, horses, machine guns, airplanes, artillery, and hand-to-hand fighting, with untold casualties but no resolution to the conflict. Changes in territory conquered remained in flux.

By March 1918, when the AEF was largely in place, the German High Command began a series of five major offensives against the French and British, designed to end the war in Germany's favor. These battles at first were effective and lethal, but by July the tide had turned in the Allies' favor. Though much fighting

---

[10]   Matthew J. Davenport, *First Over There, The Attack on Cantigny, America's First Battle of WWI* (New York: St. Martin's Press, 2015), 51-53.

and dying was still ahead, the American presence in all respects provided a major lift both in frontline combat and in morale.[11]

While Captain Ferguson was still in training in San Diego, many of these battles were underway, including the Somme Offensive (August 8–November 11, 1918), Belleau Wood (June 1918), and the Second Marne (July–August 1918). The battles of Ypres (August 19–November 11, 1918) in Belgium and Saint Mihiel (September 12, 1918) and the Meuse-Argonne (September 12–November 11, 1918) in France were yet to come but would continue the general arc of ascendancy of the Allies. American soldiers continued to provide a turning point in the outcome of these battles.[12]

But combat alone would not explain the change in fortunes of the Central Powers.

> The German Army was now being assailed by the first of the three waves of the 1918–19 influenza pandemic, which reached it some three weeks earlier than it did the Allied troops. Starting in May, the disease affected 139,000 men during June and peaked in early July. It was much less lethal than the second wave in the autumn, but it lasted for four to six days on average and even after men got over the symptoms it left them debilitated. The outbreak was one more reason why the German attack formula that had seemed all-conquering was losing its potency, while the French and British were finding answers to it.[13]

---

11   Stevenson, *With Our Backs to the Wall*, 30-170.

12   Stevenson, *With Our Backs to the Wall*,.30-160.

13   Stevenson, *With Our Backs to the Wall,* 91.

Lillian and Peter Ferguson, Harold's parents.
Ferguson Family Collection

Peter and Lillian Ferguson's Hollywood home.
Ferguson Family Collection.

Delta Kappa Epsilon Fraternity House, Stanford
University. Ferguson Family Collection.

Harold Ferguson, center, President of Delta Kappa
Epsilon, Stanford. Ferguson Family Collection

Harold Ferguson and Dolores Gordon Ferguson,
February 1916. Ferguson Family Collection

Harold G. Ferguson, 1918 just before going to
France. Ferguson Family Collection.

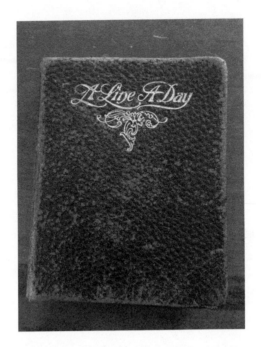

Cover of A Line A Day Diary during military
service, Ferguson Family Collection.

Sample of Diary pages 1918, 1919. Ferguson Family Collection.

American Legion Convention Medal, September
1922. Ferguson Family Collection.

Orpheum Theatre Advertisement, by Joe Duncan
Gleason. Gleason Family Collection.

Hazel Gadbury Ferguson, Third Wife, 1941.
Ferguson Family Collection.

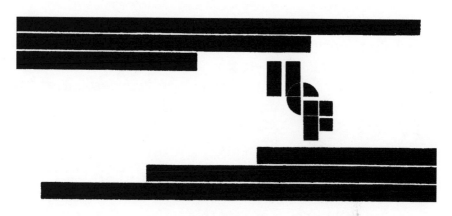

Chapter 3

Captain Ferguson Arrives in France

On August 15, 1918, Captain Harold Ferguson and his regiment, the 143rd Field Artillery of the Fortieth Division, shipped out of Hoboken, New Jersey, on the SS *Armagh*, sailing to Liverpool, England. They were surprised by the sights. At Knotty Ash, a US rest camp used during World War I, they saw the English and Scottish wounded and, most disconcerting, the absence of military-aged men on the streets. The troops reported that the restaurant food lacked fat and sugar.

From Liverpool the regiment traveled to Southampton, a rather chaotic city full of European soldiers arriving and departing daily.

> August 31, 1918: "Saw German prisoners at work—husky brutes but very much Germans. My hatred against them grows daily. Saw first [American] Red Cross ambulances hauling wounded men."

The troops boarded the ship *Charles* and arrived in Havre, France, on August 28. They immediately disembarked to a rest camp. The officers had dinner at the YMCA, their first exposure to the YMCA in France. Now they were officially part of the American Expeditionary Force in Europe! Ferguson's journal entries document his troop's movements and impressions as they traveled through France to their final destination, an artillery training camp called Camp Souge, outside of Bordeaux in the south.

September 2, 1918— "Not allowed to go [leave the ship] into Havre. Left rest camp in PM. Left Havre at 3:30 PM—men in boxcars—officers in second class coaches. Passed through Rouen—saw spires of famous cathedral L'Aigle."

September 3, 1918— "Stopped out of Le Mans for coffee where we saw many more German prisoners not doing anything, well fed and sullen. Arrived at Tours where saw first American Red Cross train full of wounded. About 40 men and Thompson left at Tours when our train pulled out. Passed Chatellerault [commune in the Vienne department in the Nouvelle-Aquitaine region in northern France] and arrived Poitiers 8:30 PM. Went to Hotel du Palais—typical French style."

September 4, 1918— "Taken to Chateaux Boivre where we are installed in very good quarters. Beautiful country surrounding and chateau very romantic with poster beds and circular stairways, high ceilings—no lights except candles."

September 7, 1918— "Went to Poitiers in AM. Many wounded French soldiers and officers. Warren and I went to cinema and saw one episode 'Patria Mrs. Vernon Castle.'" [Patria was a 1917 fifteen-chapter serial film starring Irene Castle and funded by William Randolph Hearst in the US during the lead-up to World War I.]

September 8, 1918— "Visited all important churches in Poitiers with Father Chenins including cathedral. Many women in all churches praying for fallen soldiers."

September 16, 1918— "Moved from Poitiers at 9:30 AM in 50 cars going to Cadaujac. Went through Angeuleme [*sic*] which is a very large and historic place. Arrived Bordeaux 7:45 PM. Passed tremendous American QM Base out of B[ordeaux]. Many German prisoners there. Arrived Cadaujac 9 PM—no one to meet us. Inefficient liaisons. No one knows of our coming."

September 17, 1918— "Slept in [Sam] Hover's quarters last night. Inspected billets of all of the men in the morning all of which are better than those of Poitiers. Village of Leognan progressive for a French village. Billeted in Chateau Bois-Martin in the afternoon where best quarters yet were given Colonel and myself."

September 19, 1918— "Received orders to send additional officers to Souge [Camp de Souge, near Bordeaux, was a field artillery training facility]. Saw camp and Colonel Bush of [Regiment] 134FQ62 Brig. Fair camp—many inconveniences. Much activity. Brought 2nd Lt DuBois, French Army to camp instruction."

September 23, 1918— "Inspected 2nd Bn [battalion] in AM and watched practice of band. Colonel went into Bordeaux left me in charge of camp. Col. Gundry came and ordered regiment out tomorrow for Camp de Souge. Late tonight orders for a movement of regiment via railroad or truck on Wednesday."

September 25, 1918— "Waited all morning for orders to move to Souge but could get no satisfaction until 9:30 AM when Col ordered movement by foot, distance 20 miles. 1st Bn moved out of Leognan at 12:36 PM. Regiment reached Souge 10:30 PM where they were put away in good order by Sgt. McNerney. Went back with Colonel to Chateau Bois-Martin."

September 28, 1918— "Went out to see 75 mm guns [standard 'light cannon' field gun used by French] firing on range with [soldier] Eufer. Sanitary conditions in this camp are terrible and is necessary to have special details always to keep conditions even livable. Band concert in evening."

September 30, 1918— "Started in at school for field artillery which is evidently an efficient one. All courses are of the practical character and cover some of the subjects we studied at Kearney [California National Guard training camp near San Diego]. Received material. Full regiment of 75 mm guns. First impression is not a good one but can see how mobile they must be and how simple they are in construction."

October 1, 1918— "Continued school all AM. The more I see of the manipulation of the firing data by the French system the more I am convinced it surpasses ours. The refinement to the fraction of a mil is excellent. Bulgarians breaking from fight."

October 2, 1918— "Still continuing courses at school. It is an excellent school with all instruction and the school business and practical efficiency. Some of the [Fort] Sill [School of Fire] graduates [from the US Army Field Artillery School, Lawton, Oklahoma] are not all they are cracked up to be. Think however that I can get by with the data given in school."

YMCA Overseas Service in World War I

The YMCA, along with the Salvation Army, the Knights of Columbus, and the Jewish Welfare Board, played a pivotal role in supporting soldiers during their time in Europe. The YMCA in France became Captain Ferguson's primary social support group. It seemed particularly popular with American officers of the AEF and offered meals and nighttime entertainment.

November 1, 1918—"Went to see Hank Manns and some other excellent comedians at YMCA #14."

November 29, 1918—"In evening went to YMCA #7 run by a woman, the best Y we have yet encountered conspicuous by its exceptional cordiality from the ordinary Y."

December 1, 1918—"Am worried sick about her [Dot] sweet little girl. Hope she is not sick and that everything is OK. Am terribly blue. Spent lonely, idle day around camp doing nothing. Went to YMCA in evening with Luer and heard some fairly good singing by American women."

December 17, 1918—"My heart yearns for Dot more and more each day—how can I stand this awful pressure. Am studying French to take up some of anxiety. Went to YMCA with Ezzell but rotten show came home."

December 19, 1918—"Dot bought Liberty Bond for Xmas present. Most acceptable present I could have had. Tickled me pink. Went to show at Y by 141 FA [Field Artillery regiment] in evening and surely was good for amateurs."

December 24, 1918—"In the evening went to party at YMCA. Col D sick. Xmas Eve and no Dot."

December 30, 1918—"Went to Y in evening and saw excellent show by 141 FA enlisted men. As good as professional show."

January 22, 1919—"Went to YMCA with Major [George] Burke in evening which is only entertainment we get. It is not very good usually but it affords a place to go to break the horrible monotony of accomplishing nothing."

January 28, 1919—"In evening went to Y to see picture, fairly good."

January 30, 1919—"Went to movie at YMCA Merry Makers again at Knights of Columbus bldg. Excellent."

February 25, 1919—"Had meeting to consider resolution to different governments for purpose of getting trains

through Lubiana on same basis as [American] Red Cross
and YMCA relief."

Author Richard Faulkner writes,

Going into the war, the American Army was
aware of the importance and codependence of
morale and discipline in warfare. In 1906, the
army reformer J. Franklin Bell went so far as
to lecture a group of Leavenworth students that
"the military commander who contemptuously
disregards the psychological equation of his
soldiers will never succeed on earth" …

Simply stated, morale was the unit's and its
soldiers' collective ability to more or less willingly
accept the hardships that came with military
service and the mental and moral shocks of
battle. Morale provided individuals and units the
resiliency and fortitude to endure privations and
casualties while staying focused on achieving
their missions.[14]

The soldiers had to have faith in their mission and a belief
that the people at home were supporting them in order to fight
effectively as a unit.

The army War Department wanted to provide social and
welfare support to recruits, and it understood that easing the
transition from civilian to military life would require diversions
from military training, but it needed the help of nonmilitary
groups to accomplish this.

---

[14] Faulkner, *Pershing's Crusaders*, 516–17.

In April 1917 the War Department formed the Commission on Training Camp Activities to suppress vice around training camps and offer wholesome outside activities, including movies, athletic endeavors, and canteens where trainees could get candy, cookies, and cigarettes and write letters to their families. Several welfare agencies were organized to assist in this activity. They included the YMCA, the Knights of Columbus, the Salvation Army, the American Red Cross, and the Jewish Welfare Board.

Prior to troops being sent to Europe, these organizations built several hostess huts in major American training camps and ports, where soldiers could meet with family members and friends. In general, the soldiers and families were quite happy with the home-based programs for the troops.

In France, however, the AEF could not organize a comparable social environment for the troops once they arrived. General Pershing enlisted the same organizations in France to provide social services. In August he issued General Order 26, making the Red Cross responsible for "welfare work" and assigning the YMCA (and later the Salvation Army and Knights of Columbus) to "provide for the amusement and recreation by means of its social, educational, physical and religious activities."[15] Unfortunately, the army's ocean transport system was already overloaded with men and war materiel, which took priority over welfare workers, entertainers, and nonmilitary goods.

As the YMCA set about performing its stated mission, several roadblocks seemed to reduce the organization's effectiveness and popularity with the troops. Vocal criticisms caused General Pershing to investigate this and the other organizations, but the majority of complaints were aimed at the "Damned Y." Since

---

[15] Faulkner, *Pershing's Crusaders,* 519.

the AEF could not operate canteens and stores to distribute comfort items to the men and women, the YMCA volunteered to act as the quartermaster, letting the army off the hook. What surprised the troops once the YMCA took over was that they had to pay for items that they thought should have been provided for no additional cost. Many were aware that the YMCA had been a very effective fundraiser in the US. In the eyes of many, the YMCA was behaving like a business, and this angered and confused many of the soldiers the organization was trying to please. Some of the male secretaries in the Y canteens, although fit for duty, seemed to prefer the safer role of sitting behind a desk, selling goods to servicemen just in from the front. Some YMCA canteens and shelters insisted that the soldiers watch religious films or read tracts before receiving service. The YMCA did score better marks with its service to officers and with the provided entertainment, which although spotty could be quite good at times in select Ys.

Soldiers were particularly happy with the services supplied by the Salvation Army, the American Red Cross, the Knights of Columbus, and the Jewish Welfare Board, which brought cigarettes, candy, and such to the battle lines, ignoring personal risks.

According to several entries in his diary, Captain Ferguson visited YMCAs in different locales with his fellow officers. These visits seemed to have a positive effect on Ferguson's morale, which at times was quite low when he hadn't heard from his wife, but the quality of the entertainment ran the gamut from excellent to poor.

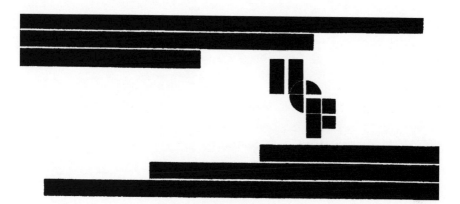

Chapter 4

Influenza Pandemic of 1917–19

I had a little bird

And its name was Enza

I opened the window

And in-flew-Enza.[16]

Although Captain Ferguson was never in a direct combat role, his duties as regiment commander exposed him to a previously unknown risk—many of his soldiers and those of other regiments were beginning to opt out of their military duties due to an unknown illness. Personal friends, including some officers, were being lost to duty because of a severe respiratory illness that no one fully understood. This protracted illness seemed to have significant morbidity in its victims, requiring hospitalization for some. Other affected soldiers did not recover.

---

[16] Francis Russell, "A Journal of the Plague: the 1918 Influenza," Yale Review, 47 (December 1947) 223-4.

August 18, 1918—"Sea still as smooth as glass and no sickness aboard except some influenza among some Tennessee recruits going as replacements—ignorant, poor specimens of manhood."

October 12, 1918—"Much Spanish influenza call 'flu' in camp. All organizations but 143 quarantined indefinitely. Men have died with same, so we are taking every precaution."

October 14, 1918—"Many more cases of Spanish influenza and cemetery just out of camp is rapidly filling."

October 21, 1918—"145 FA regiment have had 10 deaths [Spanish flu], [FA] 338, 20 from Spanish flu. Cemetery at gate rapidly filling with poor fellows dying here."

October 24, 1918—"Spanish flu is so bad that it is affecting transportation. Engineers cannot run trains. Usual French inability to meet conditions out of beaten routine. Hover has flu."

October 25, 1918—"Question of transportation for regiment after finishing [artillery] school has arisen as French have taken some trains off lines because of Spanish flu. Many dying every day."

October 28, 1918—"No deaths from flue and sick rate nominal. Only 17 to date with 2 in hospital. Only organization here not in quarantine."

October 29, 1918—"Sickness in camp going down in percentage due to strict methods used in fighting the flu. Also have overcome the bad system of sanitation and sewerage that exists in this camp."

November 1, 1918—"Heard Wilmer Grovase died of Spanish flu. Eight [FA] 144 officers in hospital with same."

The name "Spanish flu" implied that this disease had originated in Spain. But such was not the case. The name came out of press reports from a neutral Spanish press that was free to publish infection rates and other data. Combatant countries, on the other hand, did not publish such reports, not only for fear of spreading prejudicial information to other combatants but also because of their inability to control this spreading infection. The AEF did not instruct medical officers to make influenza a reportable disease until October 7, 1918.[17]

The diary's reports of illness from southwest France (Bordeaux region) constitute only a partial listing of cases of the disease; it emerged in other parts of France and Europe as well. The disease had first been reported in military training camps in the US in the early spring of 1918. The first confirmed case was reported in Camp Funston, Kansas, in Private Albert Gitchell. On March 4, 1918, mess cook Private Gitchell suddenly developed an acute respiratory illness with productive cough and fever. He recovered but was lost from duty for some time. By noon of March 11, over one hundred fellow soldiers had become ill, and within days over five hundred men had reported to sick bay. Although they lost sick time from their duties, most recovered.

By April other cases of sick young soldiers were reported at Camp Shelby, Mississippi, followed by a more virulent illness to newer recruits in June. The first group that had been infected with influenza was protected when this second wave of illness struck the camp. Captain Dwight Eisenhower reported a flu epidemic at Fort Colt, a tank training center near Gettysburg. He seems to have effectively dealt with this contagion by using strict isolation techniques.[18]

---

[17]   Faulkner, Richard, *Pershing's Crusaders,* 587.

[18]   Jean Edward Smith, *Eisenhower in War and Peace*, (New York, Random House Publishing Group, 2012), 47.

Boston, Massachusetts, hosted more flu cases, with two thousand officers and men of the First Naval District becoming ill. In these men onset of illness was sudden, leading rapidly to high fever and prostration. Fevers of 101 to 105 degrees Fahrenheit were reported within two hours. The men experienced general weakness associated with severe muscle ache, back pain, and headaches, as if "they had been beaten all over with a club."[19]

Transfer of infected soldiers from Camp Funston, Kansas (renamed Fort Riley), through the French port of Brest could have introduced the virus to the Allies in Europe. Fort Devens, near Boston, was also a shipping port for soldiers to France and has been implicated.[20]

To the soldiers, sailors, and officers of the American Expeditionary Force, the onset of flu symptoms was an unexpected setback—these young men were healthy with no significant medical conditions. In the milder first wave of contagion, symptoms consisted of body aches, fever, and cough with general weakness. Although this wave of the illness was not usually associated with serious respiratory compromise, the symptoms were enough for those afflicted to go off-duty, rest until energy returned, and then resume duties. In the later stages of the pandemic, victims experienced more severe respiratory symptoms, with dyspnea (shortness of breath) and copious mucous, along with hemoptysis (coughing of blood) requiring hospitalization. Treatment in an era without respiratory therapy or ventilators, however, remained mostly supportive. Many of these individuals contracted secondary

---

[19]   Albert Crosby, America's *Forgotten Pandemic* (Cambridge University Press, 1989), 39.

[20]   Gina Kolata, *Flu: The Story of the Great Influenza Pandemic and the Search for the Virus that Caused it* (New York, Simon and Schuster, 1999), 13-18.

bacterial pneumonia, which caused a protracted and often lethal course. This secondary pneumonia was especially difficult to treat in an era without antibiotics.

Beginning in the autumn of 1918—September through November—many victims presented with severe primary viral pneumonia characterized by acute bronchiolitis and alveolitis. Symptoms included advanced respiratory compromise with severe dyspnea, cyanosis (blueness of extremities and lips due to lack of oxygen), and uncontrollable upper-respiratory secretions, and death often came within forty-eight to seventy-two hours. This syndrome, now known as Adult Respiratory Distress Syndrome, or ARDS, is defined pathophysiologically as inflammation of small airways and alveoli (air sacs). With inflammation comes hemorrhage, overproduction of mucous, alveolar collapse, and impaired or absent air exchange (oxygen and carbon dioxide).

Some have suggested overactive immune systems present in this healthier age group to explain this catastrophic course; others have suggested that the virus became more lethal over time as it mutated. "In many places yet another severe wave of influenza hit in early 1919," a third wave.[21]

The effect of the pandemic in American units was significant during the summer battles in Belleau Wood and the Marne in June and July 1918. Further losses accelerated in AEF units during the autumn campaign in the Meuse-Argonne (September through November 1918), the result of increased lethality of the virus (the second wave of the pandemic). Replacement troops for those lost due to influenza on top of battlefield injuries were

---

[21]   Jeffrey K. Taubenberger., Ann H. Reid, "Capturing a Killer Flu Virus", Scientific American (April 27, 2009).

unavailable for General Pershing when he requested them from Chief of the General Staff March.[22]

"The military medical community was certainly caught off guard by the virulence, rapid spread, and degree of mortality of the disease. One base[camp] physician was quoted 'During the influenza epidemic we all learned a good deal about the disease ... although in the end we came out knowing as little about its bacteriology and cause as in the beginning.'"[23]

There was little that army medicine could do since doctors didn't understand the transmission and did not have the facilities to quarantine the ill. Antibiotics for secondary pneumonia were still decades from being developed. "As crowded training camps, troop ships, and frontline trenches allowed the virulent strain of influenza to spread rapidly through the ranks, the demoralized doctors were left shaken by their failure to control the disease and hesitant to question the health-related decisions of their line-officer superiors."[24]

The pandemic influenza virus appeared in different countries and populations at different times. "The data suggest that the Austrians witnessed a previously unacknowledged regional epidemic of considerable influenza-induced mortality during the first and second quarters of 1917, significantly predating the viral waves that began in the spring of 1918 in the United States."[25]

---

[22] Stevenson, *With Our Backs to the Wall*, 251

[23] Faulkner, *Pershing's Crusaders*, 587.

[24] Falkner, Pershing's Crusaders, 588.

[25] Andrew T. Price-Smith, *Contagion and Chaos: Disease, Ecology and National Security in the Era of Globalization (Massachusetts Institute of Technology, 2009)*, 74.

Germany was infected by lethal influenza in the spring of 1918: "the influenza epidemic in June and July affected more than half a million men; altogether between March and July 1918 about 1.7 million German soldiers fell ill at some point and roughly 750,000 were wounded."[26] The disease had widespread effects in the civilian population, with female civilians, including those who were pregnant, more likely to develop secondary pneumonia and tuberculosis as sequelae to the viral infection.[27]

One of the factors that increased German vulnerability to influenza infection was mass starvation, engineered by the British blockade of Germany since 1914, which stopped all foodstuffs in addition to military supplies to the civilian as well as the military population. "In late June of that year [1918], Ludendorff [quartermaster general and strategic planner for offensive battles] noted that over 2000 men in each division were suffering from influenza, that the supply system was breaking down, and that troops were underfed."[28]

Influenza infections in many German soldiers reduced battle effectiveness. Since more soldiers were dying or being hospitalized than were available to fight, morale and hope among the German troops were rapidly declining.[29] This was especially true in the last four battles of the war—Somme Offensive (21 March to 5 April 1918), Ypres-Lys (9 to 29 April 1918), Saint Mihiel (September 28–September 31,1918), and Meuse-Argonne (September 26–October 1,1918). One of the reasons for a pause in the fighting in early October was the second and deadliest wave of the influenza pandemic. This

---

[26] Price-Smith, *Contagion and Chaos*, 78.

[27] Price-Smith, *Contagion and Chaos, 79*

[28] Price-Smith, *Contagion and Chaos,80-81*

[29] Price-Smith, *Contagion and Chaos, 85*

pandemic had reached the armies in September and was in full swing by the date of the armistice.[30] Of course, it didn't help that Italy was fighting Austria-Hungary in the East in October and November 1918, meaning the Austrian Army needed German divisions to avoid annihilation. Soon Germany sued for peace (armistice). Data analyses of mortalities and morbidities during the last phases of the war support the importance of the effects of the influenza pandemic on both military and civilian populations in the ultimate request for armistice by Germany.[31]

Modern estimates are that a minimum of fifty million people worldwide died because of this pandemic. As the influenza disease spread and worsened in severity (especially in the second and third waves of the illness), hospitals, clinics, and military bases were overwhelmed by patients whose symptoms and distress became steadily more unmanageable. With the increasing lethality of the disease, morgues were unable to accommodate the increasing number of corpses.

Strategic hard fighting by the American, British, French, and Italian armies brought the war to a conclusion, but the contribution of the global influenza pandemic to winding down the war was profound, as revealed in retrospective analysis of data comparing battlefield versus illness casualties. The number of individuals who died from influenza was greater than combined combat deaths.

Two American influenza victims would become famous decades later because their deaths would open the door to the recovery of the fatal 1918 pandemic virus for research purposes. Both were young and healthy when they reported to training camps in 1918 to begin artillery training. Roscoe Vaughn reported to

---

[30]   Stevenson, David, With Our Backs to the Wall,2,2b,128-131,135,162.

[31]   Price-Smith, Andrew T., Contagion and Chaos, pp.68-73.

Camp Jackson in South Carolina, and James Downs reported to Camp Upton in New York. Both reported in September 1918, and both died in rapid succession from influenza. Vaughn reported to sick call on September 19 and died September 26, gasping for breath. An autopsy showed 300 cc of clear fluids in his chest. The entire surface of his left lung had petechial hemorrhages, and his alveoli (air sacs) were filled with fluid. A sample of his lung tissue was taken, placed in formalin, and sealed in candle wax. The sample was sent to Washington, DC, to the Armed Forces Institute of Pathology.

The AFIP originally called the Army Medical Museum was established in 1862 during the Civil War by then Surgeon General Dr. William Hammond who was chosen by President Lincoln for his experience and knowledge of medical science. Hammond was concerned about the lack of medical knowledge and effectiveness of medical officers in the field and directed in his Circular No.2 ":by careful collection and comparison of the anatomical wreckage of the great war in which the United States and Confederate States were then engaged, there might emerge a body of knowledge and understanding which, in time, lead to the lessening of human suffering and the saving of human life." [32]

James Downs reported to his base hospital on September 23 with a fever of 104 degrees, delirious and complaining of body aches. By the next day, he had become cyanotic (blue extremities and lips due to poor oxygen exchange), and he died on September 26. As in Vaughn's case, his autopsy showed lungs filled with fluid and blood. Sections of his lung were taken and, much like Vaughn's, were placed in formalin and wax and sent to Washington. [33]

---

[32] Robert S. Henry, *The Armed Forces Institute of Pathology: Its First Century* (Washington D.C.: Office of the Surgeon General, 1964), 1.

[33] Price-Smith], *Contagion and Chaos,* 29-30.

In the 1990s both lung tissue samples, which had remained in storage, would be rediscovered and would provide the few surviving samples of the pandemic virus.

The Science of the Influenza Virus

The war ended with the armistice, but influenza remained an ongoing major public-health dilemma for decades, and even today it poses substantial risks to the health of populations. Suddenly, in the decades after the war, scientists were flooded with queries and money to answer the many questions about the causative agent of this "flu" and why it was so lethal to so many individuals. The world suddenly became a more menacing place when a disease could affect young healthy individuals and have such devastating effects on a global scale.

Before 1930, the only known infectious agent remotely likely to have caused this pandemic was the bacterium *Hemophilus influenzae.* Efforts to transmit the disease using this organism in human volunteers were unsuccessful. This left scientists at a loss for where to look for this mysterious agent. The science of microbiology was still in its infancy, and a way to culture and identify the real organism had not been invented. Additionally, because the pandemic had ended in 1919 and the infected individuals had either died or recovered, there was no clinical material left from which to obtain suitable specimens.

In 1930, an Iowan pig farmer named Richard Shope, who was also a physician, made an observation that would change the course of influenza science. His swine had come down with a disease almost identical in symptoms and course to human influenza, and this epidemic had begun in 1918. The disease had spread rapidly throughout the midwestern swine population. Instead of spontaneously resolving like it had done in humans, this flu had continued to recur every year in swine throughout Europe and Asia. In 1930 Shope isolated the swine virus, A/swine/Iowa/30, three years before the human virus was isolated.[34] "Analyses of antibody titers from 1918 influenza survivors from the late 1930s, correctly suggested that the 1918 strain was an H1N1-subtype influenza A virus and was closely related to what is now known as 'classic swine' influenza virus."[35]

Jeffrey Taubenberger summarizes Shope's conclusions about the connection between the swine flu virus and the human 1918 virus:

> Swine influenza virus represents a surviving form of the human pandemic virus of 1918, and that it has not had its immunological identity detectably altered by it prolonged sojourn in hogs ... the presence in human sera of antibodies neutralizing the swine virus would be considered as indicating that the [human] donors of these sere had undergone an immunizing exposure to or infection with an influenza virus of the 1918 pandemic type.[36]

For human studies, prisoners and volunteers were unsatisfactory groups in which to study the virus. While studying dog distemper using ferrets as lab animals, researchers realized that they

---

[34] Jeffrey Taubenberger, Ann H. Reid et al "Integrating historical, clinical and molecular genetic data in order to explain the origin and virulence of the 1918 Spanish Influenza virus", Phil. Trans. R. Soc. Lond. B (2001)356, 1829-1839.

[35] R. Shope, "The incidence of neutralizing antibodies for swine influenza virus in the sera of human beings of different ages." J. Exploratory. Med. 63 (1936):669-684.

[36] Taubenberger," Integrating historical, clinical and molecular genetic data" 1829-39.

might be able to infect these animals with human influenza virus. Exposing ferrets to filtrates of mucous from flu patients eventually was successful and finally produced an animal model that could propagate the virus. By 1933 the group had isolated the human influenza virus (A/WS/33) but remained unable to culture the virus.[37]

It would not be until the 1950s that the virus could be cultured in embryonated chicken eggs. This virus was found to be a type A with genes composed of RNA (ribonucleic acid) instead of DNA (deoxynucleic acid). RNA virus genomes had been found to be less stable than DNA viruses - more likely to mutate and alter their structure when exposed to other viruses. Therefore, many questions remained knowing the capacity of the influenza virus to mutate, whether this mutability would change human populations ability to develop sustained immunity.

Researchers in the 1990s began to study the 1918 pandemic viral gene structures to answer the question of whether the original pandemic H1N1 RNA virus could mutate its genetic code sufficiently to re-enter human populations and produce additional pandemics. With time scientists believed with new tools they could map the viral genes to understand their structure and infective mechanisms, but they needed to understand the genetic makeup of the original virus to map the mutations over time. But how could they study the 1918 virus without knowing whether the original pathological specimens still contained the virus after all these years and whether these virus particles were even accessible to study? For decades the mysteries of this virus had laid buried. The researchers just had to find them.

After the museum's founding all US Army physicians were requested to send specimens, photos, case histories and

---

[37]   Kolata, Gina, FLU, p. 75.

autopsy results to the museum for study and preservation. By this time the museum had been re-named Armed Forces Institute of Pathology (AFIP). Eventually military and non-military pathologists would send their specimens to the museum as well. Some of these specimens had been retrieved by pathologists and anatomists, but many remained in storage. With the help of the archivist at AFIP, Drs. Taubenberger and Reid found seven specimens from 1918, including Roscoe Vaughn's and James Downs's small biopsy specimens of lung tissue stored in formaldehyde and imbedded in paraffin blocks!

Once these specimens were located, attempts to capture the 1918 virus could commence. To capture the genes from this unknown virus, the team had to use matrix genes or "hooks" from known viruses. After several frustrating attempts with different known viruses, they used radiolabeled hooks from a 1957 pandemic virus and were able to obtain fragments of the original 1918 virus, which appeared on x-ray pictures. The 1957 virus and the 1918 virus had homologous segments on their genes, which the team concluded proved these two viruses were related. The team then used polymerase chain reactions to copy these fragments so that they could be sequenced.

Now the researchers set to work on the lung biopsy material from Roscoe Vaughn's right lung. The reason they chose the right lung was that the gross and microscopic pathology demonstrated acute bronchiolitis and alveolitis, which was more characteristic of primary viral rather than bacterial pneumonia.[38] This case became known as 1918 case 1.

---

[38] J. Taubenberger, Ann H. Reid, Amy Craft, Karen E. Bijwaard, Thomas G. Fanning," Initial Genetic Characterization of the 1918 "Spanish" Influenza virus", Science 275 (1997):1793.

One key development in the field of human molecular genetics in the intervening years was the discovery in 1983 of polymerase chain reaction technology which allowed enzymatic amplification of targeted sequences of viral DNA. Now medical science had developed a technique to sequence genes from viral material found in autopsy and biopsy specimens from previous eras so long as these tissues had been preserved. In 1993, a group at the Armed Forces Institute of Pathology, which included Jeffrey Taubenberger and Anne Reid, began to bring polymerase chain reaction technology to identifying genetic material from the original influenza virus responsible for the pandemic of 1918.

They now set to work on resurrecting and identifying all the RNA genes (eight gene strips in all) from the 1918 culprit virus. These included genes encoding hemagglutinin, neuraminidase, nucleoprotein, matrix protein 1, and matrix protein 2. The official designation of the pandemic virus thus became A\1918\H1N1. This nomenclature was based on the specific structure of two viral surface proteins, hemagglutinin and neuraminidase. All future influenza A viruses would be categorized according to this nomenclature. These proteins muted over time since the unstable RNA genes were vulnerable to genetic shifts and drifts.

The action of the virus when infecting the human respiratory cells is initiated by the hemagglutinin protein on the viral surface (capsid) merging with a specific receptor on the human cell. This connection then allows the virus to enter the cell. In addition, the hemagglutinin (HA) protein is the primary site for action by a host's immune system. "Pandemic influenza results when an influenza strain emerges with an HA protein to which few people have prior immunity. It is thought that the source of HA genes that are new to humans is the extensive pool of influenza viruses infecting wild birds."[39] But since avian influenza has not been capable of directly infecting humans, before this virus could attach to human respiratory endothelial cells, it would have had to infect a second animal host, where gene swapping could produce a virus with specific attachment proteins on the surface to infect humans.

In 1957 a flu pandemic emerged in China, killing between one and four million people. This virus was identified as A\ H2N2\1957. In 1968 another Asian pandemic, the Hong Kong flu (A\Hong Kong\H3N2/1968), suddenly appeared, killing over one million people. This virus contained genes from avian influenza viruses. In the 2009 pandemic, the "swine flu" was found to have comparable structure to the 1918 H1N1 virus and would be the second pandemic with this organism since 1918. This 2009 H1N1 had "swapped genes from human, bird, and swine viral genes."[40]

The history of influenza suggests that humans are still immunologically unprepared for new pandemics from novel viruses. Antibiotics are now available to treat secondary bacterial pneumonia in influenza victims, and there are respiratory therapies, including ventilators and high concentrations of oxygen, to control hypoxemia (low oxygen in the blood from infections in the lung). Also, new antiviral drugs have been effective. But treatment of severe lung infection is still a major challenge, and effective influenza vaccinations are still on the horizon.

---

[39]   A. Reid.," Origin and evolution of the 1918 "Spanish" influenza virus hemagglutinin gene", Proc. Natl. Acad. Sci. 96 (February 1999): 1651-1656.

[40]   Taubenberger, "Initial Genetic Characterizations," 1793.

Recruiting Poster for U.S. Army 1917. Library of Congress.

Poster for Liberty Bonds, 1917. Library of Congress.

Re-enlistment telegram, August 2, 1917, to report to
Presidio, San Francisco. Ferguson Family Collection

Artillery Regiment, 143rd, Presidio San
Francisco, Ferguson Family Collection.

Battery A – 143rd – mess at Presidio. Ferguson Family Collection.

Bivouac at Presidio. Ferguson Family Collection.

Encampment 143rd Presidio San Francisco.
Ferguson Family Collection.

Field Artillery men, Presidio. Ferguson Family Collection.

Presidio artillery stables. Ferguson Family Collection.

Target practice, Presidio. Ferguson Family Collection.

Trench warfare practice at Presidio. Ferguson Family Collection.

Artillery transport, Camp Kearney, San
Diego. Ferguson Family Collection

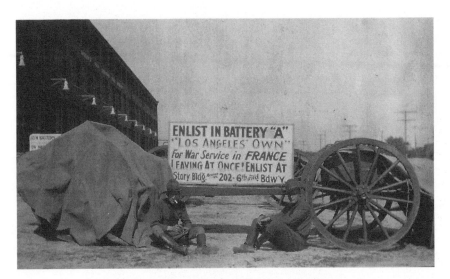

Battery A Enlistment sign. Los Angeles
California. Ferguson Family Collection.

Pre-enlistment parade, Los Angeles California.
Ferguson Family Collection.

Captain Ferguson bestowing Medals to his troops. Camp Kearney, San Diego. Ferguson Family Collection.

Silent Movie Actress Mary Pickford with Colonel Faneuff 143rd Regiment. Los Angeles. Ferguson Family Collection.

Program and Place Card for pre deployment banquet,
Jan. 31, 1918. Ferguson Family Collection.

Banquet souvenir for Harold Ferguson by Red
Cross, 1918. Ferguson Family Collection.

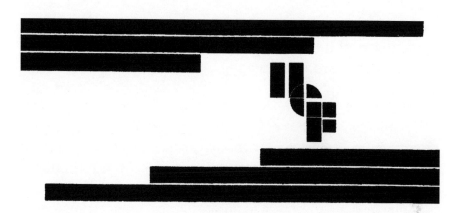

Chapter 5

The Armistice and Food Relief

In diplomacy, as in life itself, one often learns more from failures than from successes. Triumphs will seem, in retrospect, to be foreordained, a series of brilliant actions and decisions that may in fact have been lucky or inadvertent, whereas failures illuminate paths and pitfalls to be avoided—in the parlance of modern bureaucrats, lessons learned. Margaret MacMillan's engrossing account of that seminal event [in Paris in 1919] contains some success stories, to be sure, but measured against the judgment of history and consequences, it is a study of flawed decisions with terrible consequences, many of which haunt us to this day.[41]

The problem with the armistice, signed November 11, 1918, was that no fighting had ever occurred on German soil, and Germany never felt it had been defeated militarily. Hitler later

---

[41] Forward by Richard Holbrooke in Margaret Macmillan, *Paris 1919: Six Months That Changed the World.*

used this fact as a rallying cry for his Third Reich and for the undoing of the Treaty of Versailles. To quote MacMillan, "things might have been different if Germany had been more thoroughly defeated."[42]

After the signing of the armistice, Ferguson's regiment began dreaming of departing the battlefields of France to return home. Although Ferguson was anxious to return home too, the US Army had other plans for this solider who had recently been promoted to major. After being transferred from the Bordeaux region to a new regiment in northern France near Rennes (the 131 FA regiment), he decided he needed a different job description—one with more impact and fewer majors with whom to contend. On January 13, 1919, he was given a week's leave to travel to Paris, where he visited a friend, Captain Tom Gregory, who was attached to the Herbert Hoover commission overseeing food relief in Europe.

> January 13, 1919—"Decided to go see Tom Gregory about Hoover Commission and chances to get on in that work."

> January 14, 1919—"Tuesday. Cold and clear. Arrived Paris at 8:30 AM and registered at station. Went to Hotel de Louvre where Red Cross is maintaining hotel for officers on leave. Splendid accommodations for a French Hotel. Went to see Tom Gregory at Mr. Hoover's headquarters but he was in Vienna and could not return for one month. Hq [headquarters] like a jail—you cannot get near anyone without a guide. Dinner at Ciro's and show at Olympia same as our Orpheum. Same acts."

---

42 Margaret Macmillan, *Paris 1919: Six Months That Changed the World* (New York: Random House, 2001), 494.

January 15, 1919—"Wednesday clear but cold. Changed hotel to Continental as rate at Carlton was cheaper and it was nearer the Tuileries my favorite piece of scenery in Paris on a large scale. Paris still beautiful in my opinion. Saw Louvre and statues about beautiful buildings adjacent to it. Wandered about small streets of downtown Paris. Went to Continental for dinner and to Theatre Rejane where I saw Mlle Polaire advertised in NY as the homeliest woman in the world."

On January 15, Ferguson wrote a letter home to his sister Dorothy. It was very descriptive of life in Paris and compared this life to that in America:

Dear Dorothy,

I am now in Paris on a few days leave, the first real leave I have had since leaving America. Every time I come here, I like it better on account of its beauty, its history, its romance and the wonderful historical happenings that are now happening right here within its boundaries. Mother of course knows what it looks like [Lillian Prest Ferguson, Harold's mother, honeymooned in Paris and studied art with Lefebre at the Academie Julian in Paris] and what there is to see here and knows how Paris lives as she has not seen it under war conditions. Tell her that such streets as the Rue de la Paix, the rue de l'Opera, the Boulevards and all the famous streets that used to be lit up are now in darkness after eight o'clock, that its cafes close at 9:30 o'clock at night that there is still is a stringency in the use of bread and sugar and that war measures still exist. Even though the armistice has been signed the government is very strict about the use of coal, flour, and such necessities of life. But there seems to be plenty of food (if you can pay for it). Everything is terribly expensive even the ordinary things of life and those that we have at home in abundance. It is terrible these French people can painlessly extract money from you and then get you to thank them for it. It is uncanny. Tell mother also that most of the famous paintings have been removed from the Louvre and that it is closed at times to the public. I have, though, seen many beautiful works of art both oil and sculpture and wonderful architecture, so beautiful that I thought at one time it could not be built. The decorations on the top of the Notre Dame Cathedral and on the side of the Louvre actually resemble lace work; they are so fine and dainty. Of course this country at its best is no place to live in for a steady diet as their ideals, their method of living and their conditions of life are all inferior to ours.

Our brigade is now under orders to proceed home and I sincerely hope soon. There is now some talk here in Paris of some brigades that have been ordered home being sent to Russia. So far I have not received any information concerning our being included in such a catastrophe. So we may soon be on our way home. I have been looking forward to that pleasure for months now, since the signing of the armistice and hope I am not disappointed again. Once is enough.

Give my love to mother and take the best of care of that "flu" patient.

Your loving brother Harold

On February 9, 1919, he arrived in Trieste, Italy, to assume his duties as an organizer and distributor of donated food to the worst-hit regions of Europe. He described finding "Italians here attempting to dictate policy when they are very poor and many people in Istria hate them cordially."

February 10, 1919—"Ultimatum delivered to Italians that labor would have to be furnished to load cars [railroad] or other labor would be brought into Trieste. Italians discourteous to mission."

February 11, 1919—"Meeting of commission held at 10 AM at which Capt. Trovati side-stepped all issues because he said regular representative was not present.

Commission looked for offices but had trouble with Italian Colonel in command in Trieste who was actually insulting. Italians are antagonistic to work of Commission. Running out Americans. Italians very selfish."

February 12, 1919—"Meeting of commission at 11 AM. Attitude Italian government discussed fully. Tendency to deliberately put obstacles in way of accomplishing work of mission. Capt. Trovati left for Rome today to inform the government of their perilous position. Liable to have this port internationalized if conduct continues. Invited by Trovati to go to Rome but did not go because of organization of work here commencing."

February 13, 1919—"Czeck train did not leave today for Prague although cars arrived and now being loaded with flour and fats. Burke to go out with train tomorrow to Italian border to get same through. Italian transportation worst we have encountered. Trouble in store at Fiume [port city on eastern Adriatic coast] according to reports. Trouble brewing here."

February 14, 1919—"Trovati returned from Rome, expect Ginfrida [new Italian contact in region to improve functions] tomorrow. Czeck train loaded today but Italians have no engines for same. Terrible system transportation."

February 15, 1919—"Czecko Slovaks have loaded sufficient cars for their trains but no engines have arrived."

February 19, 1919—"Ginfrida has accomplished change of attitude in Italians toward mission. He is an ambitious as well as powerful politician."

February 20, 1919—"Gregory left this AM for Cattaro [other name is Kotor in Montenegro, a port town] on SS Stribbling. Capt. Fitzwilliams arrived from Vienna & reported disaster there. Investigations showed conditions same as when Gregory was there. Trains 4 & 5 left for

Prague. New schedule of trains arranged 3 per day. Gallagher advanced 10000 Kroner for expenses."

February 21, 1919—"Received word from Colonel Caraelli and from my director Czecks had stopped their engines from proceeding to Lubiana [Ljubljana, Yugoslavia]. Some trouble along the line we have been able to touch as yet. Two more trains of flour out of Trieste for Prague."

February 22, 1919—"Colonel Causey [Colonel W.B. Causey of Chicago, American representative to interallied commission] arrived with Navy representatives from Jugos and Czecks. Had conference in AM and another at 4 PM of Navy representatives. Informed there that Jugo Slavs and Italians broken relations. No possibility of getting trains via Lubiana. No trains left Trieste for Prague. Conditions critical. Serbians tore flag off Italian train and Serbian demanded withdrawal Italian consul at Lubiana."

February 23, 1919—"Hope to get some action there to relieve Jugo Slav-Italian situation. Only place where remedy can be secured. Look for some action by Gregory. Telegram received to effect that blockade was to be lift on Dalmatian Montenegrin Coast and countries occupied by associated nations on March 1st."

February 25, 1919—"Had meeting to consider resolution to different governments for purpose of getting trains through Lubiana on same basis as Red Cross and YMCA relief."

In his February 13, 1919, diary entry, Harold Ferguson described some sort of trouble in Fiume, a port city in the eastern Adriatic that Italy had claimed as its territory. This created serious political turmoil between Italian prime minister Vittorio Orlando and US president Woodrow Wilson, who was heading the 1919 Paris Peace Conference and was not agreeable to giving the Italians all the territory they were demanding, especially the port of

Fiume. This political stalemate was responsible for temporarily blocking rail transportation of food shipments to needy areas.

Italy had been part of the Triple Alliance with Germany and Austria-Hungary since 1882, agreeing to support the alliance if either of its partner countries was attacked. Since Austria had invaded Serbia in July 1914, Italy had declared itself neutral.

The Italian demands at the 1919 Peace Conference were based on the secret Treaty of London of April 1915, which had offered extensive territories to Italy for its participation with the Allies in the war. Italy, which at the time had been allied with Germany and Austria-Hungary under the Triple Alliance, had decided to join the Allies so that it could acquire this territory. Although the Treaty of London did not include the Fiume port specifically, it did offer Trieste and various sections of modern-day northern Italy, including Trentino and South Tyrol, and some parts of the Dalmatian coast. Thus, Italy had agreed to the Allied proposal declaring war on Austria-Hungary in April 1915 and Germany in 1916.

During the 1919 Peace Conference in Paris, Italy continued to hold to the Treaty of London declarations, which inflamed the conference since Wilson, Georges Clemenceau, and Lloyd George were adamantly against giving control of Fiume and more of the coast to Italy. This issue remained unsolved until 1924, when Mussolini annexed the city to Italy.[43] After the Italian laborers agreed to return to work loading food-relief supplies onto railcars, Trieste continued to serve as a major center for food relief to many parts of Europe.

On March 6, 1919, Major Ferguson received this telegram:

---

[43] Macmillan, *Paris 1919,* 301-304.

American Expeditionary Forces, Headquarters, District of
Paris. 6 March 1919. Pursuant to Telegraphic instructions
0-4539, 5 Mar 19, GHQ, Major HAROLD G. FERGUSON,
131 F.A., is assigned to duty with Mr. Herbert Hoover,
U.S. Food Administration, with station in Paris, as of 3rd
February 19. UNITED STATES FOOD ADMINISTRATION,
By Command of Brigadier General Harts: L.S. Edwards,
Adjutant General.

Although he had been working for the American Relief
Administration since February, this officially recognized
Ferguson's involvement in the food-relief mission to save
Europe from postwar famine, one of the most important food-
relief programs in American history.

History of World War I Food Relief

Herbert Hoover was an inspired choice to oversee what would
become a monumental program. He was a member of the
first graduating class at Stanford University and had become
a successful mining engineer whose intelligence, diligence,
and business connections had amassed him wealth and global
contacts. He had been raised by Quakers, which had formed in
him a personal humanitarian concern for populations affected
by the war. When he was contacted by the American consul in
London shortly after the assassination of Archduke Ferdinand,
which had caused over 120,000 Americans to be trapped in
Europe, he had quickly agreed to help the Americans find a way
out of Europe and back to the United States. Hoover readily agreed
to help. This was an individual who had become a successful
problem-solver during his managing experience with labor and
engineering problems throughout the world. He was realistic,
practical, determined, and connected, and he immediately set to
work. He acquired British pounds to pay for ship transit and other

expenses and eventually got all the Americans, many of whom were schoolteachers on holiday, back to the US.

But his work had just begun. Belgium was his next big challenge. Neutral before the German invasion, the country was now at serious risk of mass famine. Trapped between the British blockade of Germany in the Baltic and North Seas (which simultaneously blockaded Belgium) and German occupiers, the country—which normally imported 70 percent of its food—was going to starve. And since Hoover had been so efficient and capable in the handling of the American refugees in Europe, the American Citizens' Committee approached him to help with the impending food shortage in Belgium.[44]

Commission for Relief in Belgium

Faced with potentially the largest relief operation in history, Hoover tentatively agreed, which gave him time to arrange his staff, to obtain funds to purchase food primarily from America, to arrange transportation, and most importantly, to secure a safe port for delivery. Prior to accepting the job, he bought options through the Chicago commodities exchange for 10,000 bushels of wheat for delivery to Belgium.[45] What would be known as the Commission for Relief in Belgium (CRB) was on its way to a reality. The commission would later serve as a model for CARE and UNICEF.[46]

A major challenge would be finding a way to deliver food to Belgium through the British blockade and the German

---

[44]   Glen Jeansonne., *Herbert Hoover, A Life (New American Library, Penguin Random House LLC,2016),94*

[45]   Jeansonne, *Herbert Hoover,* 95

[46]   Jeansonne, *Herbert Hoover,* 96

occupation lines. The Germans agreed to provide him with an open-ended passport that read "This man is not to be stopped anywhere at any time" if he agreed not to reveal any of their military secrets. He set up CRB headquarters in London and used the neutral port of Rotterdam for food shipments from America on transport ships with a red and white "CRB" painted on the sides to protect against U-boat attacks. The British were more difficult to convince. First Lord of the Admiralty Winston Churchill accused Hoover of being a spy and requested that foreign minister Edward Grey look into the matter. When no irregularities were found, Churchill still considered Hoover an "SOB" and refused to allow his ships passage through the blockade. Hoover then appealed to Prime Minister Herbert Asquith, who overruled Churchill and allowed the relief effort to proceed.[47]

Special care for children and women was high on Hoover's list, and this included providing an extra noon meal from canteens set up in Belgium and a special free milk program for children under three years of age.

Distribution of food relief to Belgium encountered national and combatant borders and money. American volunteers combined with local French citizens in Northern France to distribute food to both Northern France and Belgium, and CRB member and Stanford professor Vernon Kellogg helped to assuage German occupants' about sending food across German borders to the needy. Convincing Britain to allow food relief to Belgium had been a hard sell, but Hoover had convinced Lord Grey that to allow previously neutral Belgium to starve would shame his country.

---

[47]   Jeansonne, *Herbert Hoover*, 100.

Although Herbert and his wife Lou were constantly campaigning to raise private funds to support these relief efforts, it became obvious that private money by itself would not be enough to continue supplying food to both Belgium and northern France. Lloyd George eventually agreed after much debate to overcome many of the British hurdles to helping with food relief and provided $4.8 million to the CRB. The French bank wrote Hoover a check for $7 million initially, with regular contributions to continue aid.[48]

As conditions in Europe continued to deteriorate, Hoover moved the headquarters of the CRB to New York. In January 1917, Germany reinstituted submarine warfare in the Atlantic, partly as a response to the British blockade, and American as well as CRB ships were attacked. This convinced Hoover to return to Europe and reestablish the headquarters of CRB in Rotterdam, turning over its operations to neutral Spain and Holland.

With the release in Washington, DC, of the Zimmerman Telegram, along with the German resumption of submarine warfare in the Atlantic, President Wilson finally agreed to declare war on Germany on April 6, 1917. Shortly thereafter, Wilson appointed Hoover director of the newly formed US Food Administration, with direct access to the president.[49]

The US Food Administration

Americans had to be convinced that supporting the troops with their hearts and minds by conserving food for shipment to starving Europe was part of their patriotic duty—eat less fats, sugar, meat, and wheat and waste less, thus providing surpluses from

---

[48] Jeansonne, *Herbert Hoover,* 109.

[49] Jeansonne, *Herbert Hoover,* 110.

their kitchen tables to send abroad. George Creel, a Progressive muckraking journalist before the war, was appointed by President Wilson to head up the Committee for Public Information. The task of the committee was to convince Americans, both native-born Americans and recent immigrants from eastern and central Europe, of the benefits of their contributions to winning the war for American democracy. Although designed to gently encourage the public, Creel's campaign became heavy-handed when he shamed those in the public who did not observe Meatless Mondays and Wheatless Wednesdays.[50]

Hoover was quoted as saying, "The question of who wins the war is the question of who can endure the longest, and the problem of endurance, in a large degree, is a problem of food and ships to carry it in."[51] He thus avoided the rancorous task of food rationing, leaving the decision to individuals who uniformly supported these efforts, and in the process he developed a new spirit of patriotism. "By a combination of price incentives and conservation the Food Administration greatly increased the export of lard, bacon, and ham to the Allies."[52]

European diets included more bread than the American diet, and Europeans were in dire need of American wheat due to the destruction of arable land in war-torn France and other Allied countries. In 1916 and 1917, drought in America had significantly impacted the wheat crop and the nation's ability to export grain. Hoover's solution was to turn to the US Grain Corporation. American wheat farmers were paid two dollars per bushel for their 1918 crop in hopes of encouraging increased production.

---

[50]   David M. Kennedy, *Over Here: The First World War and American Society* (New York: Oxford University Press, 2004), 66-70.

[51]   Jeansonne, *Herbert Hoover*,.113

[52]   Jeansonne, *Herbert Hoover*, 116.

The Food Administration also needed to find a source of sugar to meet high Allied need. But due to less than adequate supply in the US, mostly from the southern states, Hoover looked to other sources—the Philippines, Puerto Rico, and Hawaii, all of them US possessions at the time. Additionally, many of the Cuban sugar planters in the pre-Castro era were Americans. The Sugar Equalization Board was established to purchase sugar from these countries, and the US Treasury agreed to pay over $300 million to purchase sugar for the Allies. The American public was forced to endure severe restrictions in their use of sugar.

In early 1918, the Russian Revolution had taken Russia out of the war (Treaty of Brest-Litovsk), and Germany was planning a final assault on the western front to force a conclusion to the war before American troops arrived. Transportation of food to Europe was competing with shipments of American troops, but Hoover kept up food distribution to Europe with his logistical genius. Because of a ramped-up American wheat crop, Hoover planned to continue sending surplus food to Europe after the war concluded, thus preventing postwar famine and at the same time selling the remaining American wheat surplus abroad.

On November 18, 1918, Hoover sailed to Europe with urgent plans to distribute food to eastern and southern Europe. Untold numbers of Poles were in immediate danger of starvation. Prior to departure, he arranged for immediate shipment of 250,000 tons of foodstuffs to European ports for distribution to these areas.[53]

---

[53]   Frank M. Surface and Raymond L. Bland, *American Food in World War I and Reconstruction period: Operations in the Organizations under the Direction of Herbert Hoover 1914-1924* (Stanford: Stanford University Press, 1931) 24.

President Wilson sent Hoover with a "Memorandum of Arrangements with Regards to Provisioning the Populations Which Are Now or Have Been under the Domination of the Central Empires":

"1) Mr. Hoover, as United States Food Administrator, will proceed at once to Europe to determine what action is required from the United States and what extensions of the Food Administration organization or otherwise are necessary in order to carry out the work of the participation of the United States Government in this matter, and to take such steps as are necessary in temporary relief.

2) In order to expedite the movement of foodstuffs toward Europe, the War Department will undertake to purchase, in the usual co-ordination through the Food Administration during the next twenty days, 120,000 tons of flour and from 30,000,000 to 40,000,000 pounds of pork products. These foodstuffs to be shipped by the diversion of Army tonnage at the earliest possible moment that the Shipping Board arranges to be consigned to French ports for re-consignment or storage.

3) This foodstuff and any other suitable surplus supplies of the Quartermaster in Europe to be made available for distribution at Mr. Hoover's direction, it being understood that if it proves infeasible to re-ship or re-direct the steamers to the territories lately held by the Central Empires, Mr. Hoover will make arrangements for the resale

of the foodstuffs to the Allied Governments or, alternatively, to the Belgian Relief.

4) In order to facilitate administration in Washington, Mr. Hoover will set up a preliminary committee to assist the Food Administration.

5) The War Department is to purchase, inspect, pay for, load, and ship these foodstuffs in the usual manner of transmission of Quartermaster's supplies, and upon transfer from the Quartermaster's Department in Europe they are to be paid for by the buyer.

6) The American representatives in Europe are to be at once instructed by cable that the whole of the matter of the American food supplies and the establishment of a more permanent organization are to be settled by Mr. Hoover on his arrival in Europe and that the United States will take no participation in any arrangements made pending that time."[54]

The Interallied Relief Organization

Hoover was greeted by harsh realities once he arrived. Because the scope of food insecurity, mass starvation, and inadequate transportation of rescue food across so many national boundaries was so great, he needed Allied support for this mission. Allied governments, however, were not in agreement as to how his process was to proceed. They wanted to pool all the resources of the Allies and associated powers and use existing interallied relief agencies to distribute food

[54]   Surface, *American Food,.24-25.*

supplies. Also, instead of a single executive director for relief, the Allies wanted a board or committee of individuals to make the decisions on relief.

Hoover, along with the American government, strongly opposed these recommendations, feeling that putting control in the hands of a chief executive was necessary to avoid squabbles and paralysis of action. The US was not agreeable to putting distribution of its food supplies in the hands of a majority vote by foreign countries.

After three futile weeks of contentious debates, Hoover moved his operation to the Hotel Crillon in London, where he set up headquarters and recruited Belgian relief volunteers to obtain facts about food shortages in Poland, Czechoslovakia, Austria, Yugoslavia, and Romania. The results were surprising, even shocking, since populations vulnerable to mass famine were much greater than had been made public. These people needed food urgently, and President Wilson, in Paris at the time, supported the American government taking immediate action.

On December 20, 1918, a relief mission under the control of the US Army was sent to Belgrade to arrange for immediate food deliveries. Another mission was sent to Vienna and a third to Warsaw. Negotiations with the Allies suddenly improved once the data on starvation and the actions by Hoover became known. On December 31, the four associated governments agreed to establish a Supreme Council of Supply and Relief, with each country to provide two delegates. At the first meeting on January 11, 1919, in Paris, Hoover was made director general of relief in Europe.[55]

---

[55] Surface, *American Food.* p.28

By February, at the request of the American representatives, the Supreme War Council organized the Supreme Economic Council, which oversaw all the economic activities of Allied and associate governments related to the armistice. Under the Supreme Economic Council, subsections included finance, blockade, raw materials, food, and maritime transport.

In December 1918, Hoover had sent representatives to sections of Europe to evaluate the hardships. Dr. Alonzo Taylor headed a mission to Vienna and part of the old Austro-Hungarian Empire as well as some areas in the Balkans. Dr. Vernon Kellogg headed a mission to Poland. Because these individuals found such dire need in these areas, Hoover arranged for immediate transport of food relief to these countries. But these countries would need permanent missions to arrange ongoing relief shipments. With the new spirit of cooperation from the interallied agencies, these relief missions were set up and manned by representatives from the several governments.

The American Relief Administration

The armistice did not end the problems of insecure food, mass famine, and disease in Europe. In fact, the British blockade of the North and Baltic Seas, with its restriction of food to noncombatant men, women, and children, continued until March 1919. Some Allies were convinced they could starve Germany and Austria into signing a punitive peace, and French minister Georges Clemenceau continued to fight for harsh sanctions against Germany and German trading partners, including restriction of food supplies. But Herbert Hoover, who had attended the Versailles conference as an aide to President Wilson, had a more humanitarian view based in part on his Quaker upbringing. In December 1918, with Hoover's prompting, President Wilson requested a hundred-million-dollar food relief appropriation from Congress:

> In pursuance of an Act entitled "An Act providing for the relief of such populations in Europe and countries contiguous thereto outside of Germany, German-Austria, Hungary, Bulgaria and Turkey, as my be determined by the President as necessary" approved February 24, 1919, I hereby direct that the furnishing of foodstuffs and other urgent supplies and the transportation, distributing and administration thereof provided for in said Act, shall be conducted under the direction of Herbert Hoover, who is hereby appointed Director General of the American Relief Administration with full power to determine to which of the populations named in said Act the supplies shall be furnished and in what quantities, and further to arrange for reimbursement so far as possible as in said Act provided.
>
> He is hereby authorized to establish the American Relief Administration for the purpose of carrying out the provisions of said Act and to employ such persons and incur such expenses as may be necessary for such purpose, to disburse all sums appropriated under the aforesaid Act or appoint a disbursing officer with that power, and particularly to employ the Food Administration Grain Corporation, organized under the provisions of the Food Control Act of August 10, 1917, as an agency for the purchase, transportation and

distribution of foodstuffs and supplies to the populations requiring relief.[56]

The American Relief Administration (ARA) would administer food and medical aid to Europe and Russia until 1924.

The ARA faced many roadblocks in distributing food to the starving populations of Europe. The transportation systems within Europe were in poor repair. This included the major rivers, canals, and railroads. Since each country emerging from the war had its own rail lines, the track gauges for individual countries often did not match, requiring full trains transporting foodstuffs across national boundaries to stop, unload, and reload onto local trains. Locomotives were in short supply and frequently remained idle due to coal strikes. Additionally, labor strikes in Trieste by workers who wanted payment in local lire instead of kroner kept empty railcars sitting on sidings.

The Paris peace negotiations were not going well for Italy since President Wilson refused to approve giving land on the eastern Adriatic (port of Fiume) to Italy. With Hoover's political expertise, these blocks were eventually opened, once lire were paid to the laborers, allowing railcars to be loaded and food distributed.

To solve the coal strikes, Hoover called on the expertise of Anson C. Goodyear, who was described as the "best coal man in the world." Goodyear doubled coal production for central Europe within one month, kept coal miners happy with supplies of tobacco, and helped establish the European Coal Administration to stabilize coal production and distribution within Eastern Europe.[57] Hoover and Goodyear built new rail lines, increased the number and availability of locomotives, and rebuilt

---

[56]   American Relief Administration Bulletin, Paris France, 17 Mar 1919.

[57]   Jeansonne, *Hoover, A Life,* 129-31

barge canals on the Danube. The ARA also built hospitals, ports, warehouses, schools, and telegraphs. "In most nations, the United States furnished only the food and a blueprint of organization, [and] volunteers at the local and regional levels implemented the program, minimizing overhead costs."[58]

A typhus epidemic, independent of the influenza pandemic, broke out in Russia in 1919 and spread through eastern Europe, involving Lithuania, Poland, Romania, Serbia, and Ukraine. Lack of soap (which had been eaten during periods of starvation), consumption of infected cats with lice, and homelessness were to blame. Hoover and the ARA were tasked with solving this potentially lethal infection, which was killing 100,000 people weekly. The ARA mobilized its forces and drew a quarantine line across Europe. Volunteers from the American Red Cross and US military personnel clipped hair and shaved heads, bathed and scrubbed the infested individuals, and burned their clothes, and within six months the effort brought an end to the epidemic, saving countless lives.

In July 1919, the ARA had officially entered the reconstruction period, meaning it no longer relied on US government funds but became instead a charitable organization that relied on private donations and sales of food to foreign relief organizations. This phase lasted until 1924, was primarily aimed at central Europe and Russia, and encompassed the European Children's Fund.[59]

---

[58]   Jeansonne, *Hoover A Life,* 130.

[59]   Surface, *American Food,* 122-24.

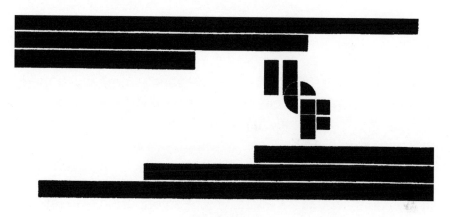

Chapter 6

Harold Ferguson Comes Home

US Army Major Harold Gale Ferguson returned home to Los Angeles in June 1919, anxious to reunite with his wife, Dolores and make his own decisions about his future.

June 21, 1919—"Arrived SF [San Francisco] 11:15 AM and went to Clark Hotel. Wonderful to be home even though in hotel with Dot [Dolores]. Saw mother [Lillian Prest Ferguson]. Dorothy [sister] to be married next Wednesday. Received telegram disapproving my expenditures for leave. Dot would not go to SF [Presidio where he mustered out of the army] with me so left alone on 6:15 PM. Tired of travel. Due to phone strikes cannot get in touch with anyone."

On June 23 he received his discharge papers from the Presidio and took the Southern Pacific overnight to Los Angeles, where he arrived at 10:15 a.m. He and his wife who had returned home while he officially resigned from the army, rented a flat at 1438 Los Palmas in Hollywood and installed furniture he had kept in storage since leaving for France. His rent was forty dollars but did not include water. "My prospects worry me," he writes.

After applying for a job at a title insurance company, he tried for employment at the city prosecutor's office. He was told his prospects weren't good. Apparently, jobs left behind during the war had been filled by those who did not serve.

Eventually, he was told of temporary employment as a lawyer in the county counsel's office, where an opportunity to replace someone on leave had opened up. He was to handle county legal matters and industrial claims against the county. Starting salary was $185 monthly.

> July 5, 1919—"Worked in office [county counsel] in morning getting acquainted with new work. The same is very congenial due to class of men in the office ... do not know how long it will last ... Looking for other openings."

> July 6, 1919—"The pleasure of doing as one cares to do was a new one and certainly delightful. There is no pleasure as great as establishing a home and using it properly."

By July 10 his salary had been increased to $275 per month, and he had begun to see the office as "a stepping stone to better opportunities."

> July 13, 1919—"Jack McDowell [real estate agent] called in evening talked over happenings since I have been gone [managing two houses owned by his mother, one on Citrus and one on June Street in Hollywood]. Went for walk to see both houses. Building progressing rapidly in neighborhood [region of Grauman's Chinese Theatre and modern-day Hollywood Bowl]."

1919 Los Angeles Railway and Pacific Electric Strikes

August 15, 1919—"Strike threatened on PE [Pacific Electric] and LA Rys [Los Angeles Railway] on account of demand of employees for exceptional increases in wages. For PE demand of raise to $180 per month for platform men."

August 16, 1919—"Strike commenced this AM at 2 AM. Some yellow cars running but very few red cars. No trouble getting to and from city on account of automobiles."

August 18, 1919—"Cars running on all lines [PE and LA Rys] although not very frequently. Sympathy of public not with the strikers."

August 22, 1919—"Switchmen on steam lines have struck because of P.E. employees claims—in sympathy. No sympathy from general public whose interests they absolutely ignore. Street car service on Hollywood line improved. Very fair service maintained on all lines."

August 23, 1919—"More cars running both on PE and LA Ry SP [Southern Pacific] now striking with other steam roads. Sympathetic strike. Dot and I went to her folks' house. No cars running coming home. Took jitney."

August 24, 1919—"Steam railroad employees by striking have tied up about $500,000 worth of fruit and food stuffs in yards. They are outlaws as brotherhoods have not authorized strike."

August 25, 1919—"Saw Deke at noon who told me about car inspectors on railroads going back to work."

Although Major Ferguson was only mildly inconvenienced by the combined railroads strike, the labor action would have major consequences for transportation and labor relations in Los Angeles. The August 1919 Los Angeles Railway (yellow car) and Pacific Electric (red car interurban) strike was the result of a unionized labor movement against employer Henry E. Huntington, who refused to recognize unions and workers' demands for better pay and an eight-hour workday.

The increased cost of living following the end of World War I created a problem for railway workers, whose purchasing power couldn't keep up with inflation since "pay raises" from the company were inadequate. In addition, rail workers routinely worked excessive hours in order to meet their workloads and had little time off. Relief from long working hours remained a nonstarter with employers, who benefited from open-ended work shifts.

In July 1919, in an attempt to head off a strike, the company increased pay for conductors and motormen and raised the beginning salary of platform men. The railway continued to resist efforts by the rank and file to engage in collective bargaining. The Los Angeles Railway agreed to talk to nonunionized employees but also hired additional managers trained to operate streetcars and additional law enforcement officers, should a strike arise.

On August 16, 1919, one-third of the streetcar motormen and conductors walked off the job. With the additional nonunion workers and law enforcement, the strike was broken by mid-September, and Henry Huntington's open-shop policy remained in force. In a speech to the New York Chamber of Commerce in 1922, Huntington said, "There would be but little difficulty between the employer and the employed if it was not for the pernicious influence of men who seek to control all workingmen, and so control the industries, and so control the country."[60]

---

[60]   William B. Fredericks, "Capital and Labor in Los Angeles: Henry E. Huntington vs. Organized Labor, 1900-1920," Pacific Historical Review 59, No.3 (1990): 394-5.

The Pacific Electric three-thousand-man strike went into effect at 2:00 a.m. on August 16 as well. The combined strikes of these two rail lines turned out to be the greatest transportation shutdown in the history of Southern California. The Mexican track layers walked out in large numbers in solidarity with the union. In the early 1900s, Mexican laborers had been brought across the border to help build the Pacific Electric railroad, and the number of Mexican workers had increased during 1917–18 because of labor shortages due to the war.[61]

After being denied unionization rights, the eight-hour workday, and adequate wage hikes, the strikers staged a violent protest in Los Angeles on August 20, 1919, against Huntington's open-shop policy, which allowed employers to hire workers regardless of union status. Strikers sabotaged streetcars by greasing their wheels and pushing them over. The strike was subdued by a local armed police force.

In response, the US naval commander sent sailors to board red cars and threaten the conductors. The city also served injunctions declaring that workers had agreed to open-shop policies when they were employed and that the employees' demands to unionize were illegal. The strikers eventually walked away with a pay increase, but the open-shop policy remained in force.

This strike action thus became one of the first indications that a growing and aggressive Los Angeles labor movement would face coordinated and violent conflict with a conservative business community that both loathed and feared liberal socialist takeover of the community. Huntington, the Merchants and Manufacturers' Association of Los Angeles, and Harrison Otis,

---

[61] Kevin Starr, *Endangered Dreams: the Great Depression in California* (New York: Oxford University Press, 2004), 64.

publisher of the *Los Angeles Times*, would remain implacable foes to attempts to replace the open-shop system in the city.

Henry Huntington, who was the largest employer in postwar Los Angeles at the time, had little interest in improving the situation for workers, especially if it meant dealing with the growing union movement. Huntington's anti-labor ("no concession to labor") policy evolved from the Pullman Palace Car Company strike of 1894. George Pullman had built a village for his employees to live in while constructing his company's comfortable sleeping cars to carry cross-country passengers. As a result of an economic downturn in 1890, Pullman severely reduced the wages and benefits to his employees, who elected to join the newly organized American Railway Union (ARU), whose president was Eugene Debs. To make the most impact, this strike called by the ARU targeted all trains instead of just those carrying the Pullman cars.[62] The action had a direct effect on the Southern Pacific railroad, owned by Henry Huntington's uncle, Collis Huntington. Henry was virulently against turning over the running of the SP railroad to a union, and this anti-labor sentiment continued once he came to Los Angeles.[63]

In July 1894, when federal troops sent by President Grover Cleveland broke up the strike, Debs was arrested and sent to prison for a three-year term. While he was in prison, his political beliefs underwent a transformative shift, leading him to become America's foremost socialist. After his release, he played a pivotal role in the founding of the International Workers of the World, a radical socialist union chartered in 1905 in Chicago.[64]

---

[62] Friedricks, William B., *Capital and Labor in Los Angeles: Henry E. Huntington vs. Organized Labor, 1900-1920,* Pacific Historical Review 59(3) pp 375-95.

[63] Fredricks, *Capital and Labor,* 380.

[64] Stevens, *Radical L.A.,* 23-25.

Debs ran for president on four separate occasions, first in 1900, then in 1904, and again in 1908. In 1912, running as the Socialist Party candidate, he received 897,011 votes. His candidacy would remain a seminal event in American labor history.[65]

The Amalgamated Street Railway Association Division 835 tried to organize the workers of the Los Angeles Railway in 1915, but without luck since the company threatened to fire any worker who joined the union. The union continued to try various strategies to unionize the railroads, and the organization's vice president, Ben Bowbeer, moved to Los Angeles from San Francisco to add heft to the action. In 1917, encouraged by the federal government and Woodrow Wilson's support of workers' rights to organize for better pay and reduced work hours, the union continued to push. In 1918 the union asked the National War Labor Board (NWLB) to intervene in the dispute. The Los Angeles Railway continued to reject any national efforts to regulate its company, repeating its contention that this was a state issue, outside the purview of the federal government. The railway continued to refuse to abide by the NWLB's recommendations.

1919 Baseball World Series

One of the great sources of entertainment for LA residents was the national game of major league baseball. Although radio and television broadcasting of games was still in the future, fans followed the games by attending ballparks and reading newspaper reports the morning after the games. The 1919 World Series, the first game of which was to start shortly after Harold arrived home, would become one of the most controversial series in history.

---

[65] Chamberlain, *Farewell to Reform*, 83

October 1, 1919—"Busy on bail bond suits. Also started work on suit on contract against City of Los Angeles for some $100,000. First game of the world's series in baseball played at Cincinnati [Redland Field]. Score 9–1 in favor of Cincinnati. Had meeting of Hollywood Post American Legion executive committee."

October 2, 1919—"Second game of world's baseball series [Redland Field]. Cincinnati won 4–2."

Not recorded in Harold Ferguson's diary were games 3 and 4. On October 3, in the third game, the Chicago White Sox won 3–0 at Comiskey Park in Chicago. On October 4, in the fourth game, the Cincinnati Reds beat the Chicago White Sox 2–0 at Comiskey.

October 6, 1919—"Cincinnati won 5th game [Redland field] 5–0 thereby winning pool for myself."

October 7, 1919—"Chicago won [sixth game at Comiskey] 5–4."

October 8, 1919—"Chicago won [seventh game at Redland Field] 4–1."

October 9, 1919—"Cincinnati winning [eighth game at Comiskey Park] 10–5."

The World Series between the American League Chicago White Sox and the National League Cincinnati Reds was of great interest in Los Angeles to all strata of society. Enthusiastic adult and teenage fans eagerly read daily morning papers for game outcomes and player performances. In 1920, however, it was revealed that the result of the 1919 series had been undermined by Chicago players intentionally throwing games, enticed by gamblers' under-the-table money.

Eight Chicago White Sox players were indicted following the loss of the 1919 World Series to the Cincinnati Reds, and although they were found not guilty, the players were permanently barred from professional baseball by the new independent baseball commissioner, Kennesaw Mountain Landis, who was hired as a result of this scandal. The White Sox owner, Charles Comiskey, had lost favor with his players when he underpaid them and gave the players only flat champagne for winning the playoffs, in place of a bonus.

Baseball players were not represented by a union and had historically had to accept owners' decisions on personnel, working conditions, and salaries. In 1919 attitudes about this had changed, and the players, like employees in many industries in Los Angeles and nationally, reacted to "unreasonable" employers demands with a growing willingness to register their dissatisfaction and promote their employment rights.

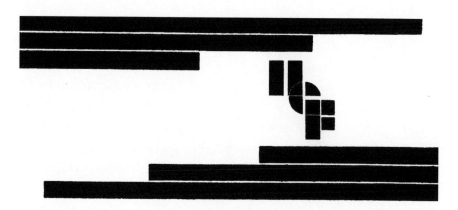

Chapter 7

The American Legion

The American Legion was just beginning to organize as the armistice ended the fighting in Europe. This group would represent all veterans in dealing with many issues that developed once the war was finished and postwar recovery was beginning. This organization was democratic in its plan and encouraged all who had served in the armed forces to join and support its efforts to ensure proper recognition of veterans' needs.

In spite of the armistice and the end of combat, morale among large numbers of veteran troops was low—their return from Europe had been delayed due to difficulty finding transportation back across the Atlantic, and there was concern about rumors of turmoil at home caused by revolutionary Russian Bolsheviks who had come to America and radical labor unions, including the International Workers of the World (IWW), that were threatening the business communities in California and elsewhere. Veterans urgently needed an organization that would stand up to such threats and remind America what they had fought for—a pure Americanism.

Other pressing needs also had a negative impact on morale. Many worried about what kind of hospital care and physical rehabilitation would be available for returning injured soldiers once they arrived in the US. Unemployment was projected to be high among veterans, and there was concern about ability to find decent jobs that could provide the vets a satisfactory lifestyle. A powerful veteran organization could help overcome barriers with employers who were reluctant to hire returning veterans. Monthly stipends might help tide veterans over until they could obtain gainful employment. Such an organization could refer potential employees for job training in nonmilitary occupations and even help with job applications and interviews with businesses seeking applicants with certain unique skills.

But before all this could be accomplished, a powerful nonpolitical private assembly of those who had served in the AEF had to be organized and formed into an institution. This would enable a group of like-minded individuals who had fought for their country to be more successful when dealing with the power structure in Washington, DC. Following the defeat of the Confederacy in the Civil War in 1865, the North had formed the Grand Army of the Republic (GAR), a successful organization of veterans that dealt with postwar concerns for Northern soldiers. The same kind of organization—a GAR of World War I—seemed to be the best model to follow as a general blueprint for World War I veterans.

The first meeting of this new organization coalesced in a rented YMCA building in Paris, France, in January 1919. The planners wanted the initial meetings to be open to all who had served with the AEF and sought to give equal voice to officers and enlisted personnel. Once the meeting became known through word of mouth throughout the military, personnel came with interest and enthusiasm from all over Europe to attend the caucus in the first phases of the organizational planning.

The attendees were not shy about participating and made their needs and views known to the assembled group. There was plenty of room for disagreement, individual speeches, questions, and commentary from the floor, but shared aims rather than obstructionism seemed to be the priority.

Theodore Roosevelt Jr., son of the twenty-sixth president, had been one of the first to talk about forming such an organization while he was still in France, and once the preliminary steps had been undertaken to inform and include the European AEF in the process, he returned to the US to spearhead a stateside organization in St. Louis in May 1919. The attendees at this St. Louis caucus were mostly those who had served in America. This caucus was less exploratory than the one in Paris and more oriented to accomplishing specific goals. An advance committee had met to divide the business into subcommittees, to cover such matters as credentials, resolutions, naming, bylaws and declaration of principles, a constitution, an emblem, permanent headquarters, and finance. Roosevelt agreed to be the temporary chairman.

Membership in what would be officially titled the American Legion—reminiscent of the earlier preparedness American Legion of 1915, which had been disbanded—would be open to all who had performed military service between April 6, 1917, and November 18, 1919, including officers and enlisted members of the AEF. Eventually, organizations from previous conflicts could be merged with the Legion. Nonpartisanship was a founding principle: "it shall be absolutely nonpolitical and shall not be used for the dissemination of partisan principles, or for the promotion of the candidacy of any person seeking public office or preferment. No candidate for or incumbent of a salaried elected public office shall hold any office in the American Legion or in any department or post thereof."[66]

Article 4 of the National Constitution, drafted at the St. Louis caucus, gave executive authority of the American Legion to the executive committee. What remained unsettled was the role of state and local organizations in enlisting members who would work to support and spread the message of the Legion. During the summer caucus of the Legion in Paris, these questions were entertained and resolved. State and local organizations were strongly encouraged, and no restrictions were placed on the size of these groups. With so many troops still located in military installations in Europe and the US, establishing "posts" in these areas and on college and university campuses was encouraged. These posts were not to come under either military or government supervision. Although uniformity of philosophy and belief was an ultimate goal, the Legion strongly urged local autonomy of local and state organizations. "Home rule is the keynote to the whole situation."[67]

The summer caucus of 1919 in Europe resulted in several key advances for the Legion. First and foremost was obtaining a charter that would not bind the organization to political oversight or control. Second, a new energy to pursue veterans' rehabilitation was emerging out of discussions with the executive committee. Positions on national defense and foreign relations were under discussion, and in anticipation of the first national convention in November on the anniversary of the armistice, a national magazine was published to advertise the Legion's work. *The American Legion Weekly*, published by Legion headquarters in New York City in July, would help to

---

[66]　Thomas A. Rumer, *The American Legion: An Official History* (New York: M. Evans and Company, Inc., 1990), 55.

[67]　Rumer, *The American Legion*, 62.

bind together a far-flung network of veterans who had no idea what the Legion stood for or could do for them.

The first issue of the *Weekly* summed up the American Legion's mission:

> Out of their common experiences through the dark months of the war has grown a comradeship and patriotism which are vitalized by their organization into this single concrete force which will stand always as a barrier against the forces of greed, ignorance, and chaos. The American Legion is the epitome of that Americanism for which it stands. Its voice is the majority voice of its members; its will the will of many. Spontaneous in inception, it has been democratic in its development.[68]

After the conclusion of the first American Legion national convention in Minneapolis in November 1919, many of the hopes and dreams of the new organization were firmed up, and programs and policies began to be established. Specific goals for the Legion included helping physically and economically handicapped veterans, promoting patriotism, and working toward a national military policy.

The national executive committee of the organization formed a post-convention meeting to accomplish the following goals: (1) "mutual helpfulness whereby all our comrades who have been handicapped in mind, body, or position through service to their country may receive that liberal consideration which they have reason to expect from a grateful and patriotic nation"; (2) "protection for our country from foes without," with the Legion

---

[68]   Rumer, *The American Legion,* 74.

"endeavor[ing] to assist in the adoption of a military policy which will make it safe from future aggression and yet a policy which will be truly democratic, truly American, just, and equitable for the entire country"; and (3) "protection for our country from foes within. Our stand for one hundred percent Americanism will be virile. As soldiers ... and now civilians ... with ever keener sense of the responsibilities of citizenship, we shall not hesitate. Now our orders originate from the constitution of the United States as expressed through the duly constituted agencies of national, state, and local government. [We will] support civilian authority and cooperate with the 100 million loyal and patriotic Americans to promote one hundred percent Americanism."[69]

American Legion in Los Angeles

Soon after his return from Europe, Harold Ferguson became aware of a community of fellow veterans in Hollywood with whom he felt a strong connection. Some were friends, others acquaintances, but all shared a common bond and history and felt alone and unsure of where to turn. This realization prompted him to consider a veterans' affairs group designed to minister to these needs. Connection with the newly organized American Legion, which was being publicized in its magazine the *American Legion Weekly*, seemed a viable solution.

Ferguson attended a meeting to discuss veterans' issues on July 21, 1919, in Wilcox Hall on Hollywood Boulevard. The meeting, headed by American Legion comrade Taylor Duncan, involved selecting a committee to apply to the National Legion for a permit to form a local charter, and Ferguson was selected for this committee.

---

[69] Rumer, *The American Legion, 114-115.*

July 21, 1919—"In evening attended meeting of Hollywood service men. Very unsatisfactory due to poor executive ability of temporary chairman."

August 4, 1919—"Went to service men's meeting in Hollywood with Jack [McDowell] and Reynolds [EM Reynolds]. Doherty Harris and Reynolds spoke to men. Better meeting than last time."

August 18, 1919—"Went to meeting of Hollywood service men with Jack and Ed Gorley. Speakers did not appear."

September 15, 1919—"In evening went to meeting of American Legion Hollywood Post. Election of officers resulted as follows. Myself president."

September 24, 1919—"Meeting in evening of executive committee of Hollywood Post. Most ambitious plans on foot now to boost this organization."

September 28, 1919—"Spent time studying and working on details for Hollywood Post American Legion. Latter should be first in the country and most influential. Mother, Dot and I went to Orpheum in evening where we saw good bill."

October 4, 1919—"Same [Amer Legion] is occupying much of my time but I consider same very important work both for service men in Hollywood and nation at large. Finished *Joan of Arc* by Mark Twain reading of places I have visited."

October 13, 1919—"Columbus day fell upon a Sunday. Secured services of Cassins Gay for American Legion. Went to Legion meeting in evening. Houdini entertained us. Victory Post executive committee out to visit up. Very good meeting by crowd."

October 31, 1919—"Executive meeting of Am Legion in evening at Hotel Hollywood."

November 11, 1919—"Went into city to Exposition Park to Armistice Day celebrations. Given by city. Received American flag presented by Anita Baldwin to Hollywood Post. Large crowd present. Brinkops, Montague and Goss represented their posts, beside myself. Governor Stephens [William], Snyder [Mayor Meredith], Capt. Riddle from Navy and others spoke. Enthusiastic gathering.

November 12, 1919—"Four American Legion men killed by IWW at Centralia Washington."

November 13, 1919—"Mass meeting of Los Angeles Post American Legion at Trinity Auditorium. Jack and I went. Splendid enthusiasm in organizing an emergency organization to fight IWWs."

November 14, 1919—"Had meeting of Hollywood Post Am Legion and formed intelligence bureau of whole post to assist authorities in running down IWWs."

Ferguson was instrumental in obtaining the charter on August 25, 1919, and was subsequently elected to serve as the first commander of the Hollywood Post, No. 43, on September 15, 1919. He was reelected twice to the same position. He wrote the first ritual, the one still used today, for the presentation of the colors and the opening of post meetings. This Legion post thus became and remained a major focus and commitment throughout his life.

His collection of medals would include "American Legion Post Commander No. 43, 1920 and 1921," "3rd Annual Convention of the Department of California American Legion in Yosemite Valley in 1921," "American Legion Convention September 1922," "Delegate to the American Legion State Convention, Santa Cruz Calif., 1924," "Delegate to the American Legion Department of California Seventh Annual Convention September 15, 1925," and "18th Department Conv, Hollywood August 8, 1936."

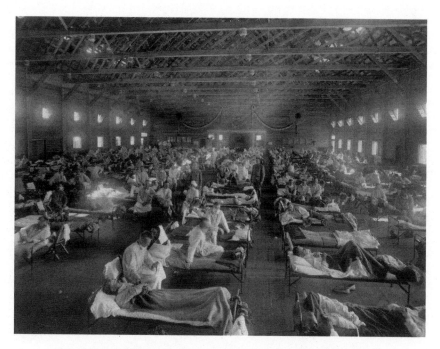

Emergency Hospital at Camp Funston Kansas 1918.
National Museum of Health and Medicine

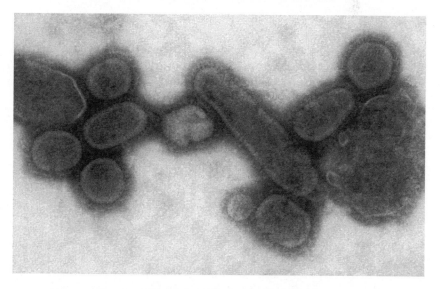

Reconstructed "Spanish Flu" virus, photomicrograph.
National Museum of Health and Medicine.

Red Cross litter carriers, "Spanish Flu" Washington D.C. 1918. National Museum of Health and Medicine.

Police practicing oral hygiene during influenza epidemic, Seattle Washington, National Museum of Health and Medicine.

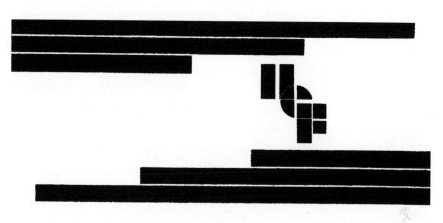

Chapter 8

Organized Labor in Southern California

Much of Los Angeles's labor history had taken place prior to Harold Ferguson's youth and while he was serving in the National Guard and Europe during World War I. Massive immigration to the US had almost doubled the country's population after 1890. Most of these individuals had emigrated from countries of origin in southern and eastern Europe, and they entered the US through New York's Ellis Island, which opened in 1892. This influx included four million Italian Catholics, 500,000 Orthodox Greeks and Catholic Hungarians, and many Catholic Poles. Other immigrants included two million Jews from Russian-controlled Poland, Ukraine, and Lithuania, along with Slovaks and Catholic Slavs from Byelorussia, Ruthenia, and Russia. Millions of southern Slavs, including Muslims, Catholics, and Jews, came from Romania, Croatia, Serbia, Bulgaria, and Montenegro.[70] This influx started the labor movement in the United States, but it didn't create a stir or have an impact on the West Coast.

---

[70] Kennedy, *Freedom from Fear*, 13.

The American census of 1930 showed 123 million people, of which 10 percent were of foreign extraction. These newly arrived ethnic migrants settled mostly in urban and industrial areas in the Northeast, where unskilled jobs were plentiful. Everywhere, newly arrived immigrants formed communities within communities to preserve their common identities and language, but most wished to adopt American citizenship and values. "The Jewish ghettoes and Little Italys and Little Polands that took root in American cities became worlds unto themselves. Immigrants read newspapers and listened to radio broadcasts in their native languages."[71]

This influx of unskilled multilingual individuals created congested, competitive urban centers where workers struggled to find adequate-paying jobs to support families in clean and safe living conditions. Because there were so many looking for work, employers in this period could pay low wages and force their workers to work twelve-plus-hour days without days off or adequate rest time between shifts. Accident rates in some industries were high due to general fatigue and monotonous repetitive work that produced loss of concentration. "Not until 1923 did United States Steel Corporation grudgingly abandon the twelve-hour day, its grinding human damage made worse by the periodic 'turnover' of the night and day gangs when the men were required to stand a continuous twenty-four-hour shift."[72] The increasing number of strikes beginning in 1914 was related to the large number of immigrants who had brought the concept of European unionism with them. Labor strikes were new to the American labor system and created conflict between the business communities and the workers.

---

[71]   Kennedy, *Freedom from Fear*, 14-15.

[72]   Kennedy, *Freedom from Fear*, 23.

Labor Turmoil in Los Angeles

The growing influence of organized labor in Gilded Age industries in the East and Midwest was not a factor for Los Angeles, which was geographically and politically isolated from the rest of the country. The completion of the Southern Pacific railroad in 1876 opened the first railway connection to Los Angeles. Migrants to Southern California included unemployed Chinese and out-of-work gold miners following the end of the Gold Rush. By 1886 the Santa Fe railroad had entered Southern California, igniting a rate war between the two railroads and drastically reducing rail fares to the region from all over the nation. By March 1887 the Santa Fe railroad was advertising cross-country travel for one dollar per passenger. "The result of this war was to precipitate such a flow of migration, such an avalanche rushing madly to Southern California as I believe has no parallel," says writer Carey McWilliams.[73] Many were retirees and the sick who dreamed of a warm and healthful life.

Tourists and sick retirees were not the only newcomers to relocate to Los Angeles from other parts of the country. Union organizers who represented unions in the Midwest and East Coast had discovered a growing population of workers ripe for representation against heartless employers. Thus, organized labor began to confront nonunion employers, demanding better wages and working conditions in a city with a well-publicized, strong anti-union history. The year 1919 would earn a reputation among historians as the worst year in the nation's history for labor strikes.

> Not only the volume but the character of immigration into southern California presented

---

[73] Carey McWilliams, *Southern California an Island on the Land* (Salt Lake City: Gibbs M. Smith Inc., Peregrine Smith Books, 1983), 118.

a grave obstacle to the development of a labor movement. The growing community, with its much advertised mildness of climate and easy living conditions, attracted wealthy folk who wished to retire, sick persons in search of health, farmers seeking a less backbreaking life, small businessmen desirous of establishing themselves, mechanics and unskilled laborers looking for high wages and year-round jobs, and finally, vagrants escaping rigorous weather in other sections. In all these groups there must have been a sizable proportion predisposed against or neutral to unionism.[74]

In addition, laborers in large numbers arrived from Mexico seeking employment in the oil, agricultural, and entertainment industries.

The city's anti-union attitude—which became known as "open-shop"—may have begun with the *Los Angeles Times* and General Harrison Gray Otis, who took over the newspaper as its publisher in 1882. A printers' strike by the International Typographical Union in 1880 has been described as "the most significant event in the history of Los Angeles labor relations before 1910 … It is clear that the 1890 strike was the beginning of a period of almost continuous conflict between the printers and the *Times* that would culminate in the open-shop wars of the early twentieth century."[75]

---

[74] Grace H. Stimson, *The Rise of the Labor Movement in Los Angeles* (Berkeley and Los Angeles: University of California Press, 1955), .102.

[75] Errol Wayne Stevens, *Radical L.A.: From Coxey's Army to the Watts Riots, 1894-1965* (Norman Oklahoma: University of Oklahoma Press, 2009), 36-38.

By 1886, Otis had purchased the paper and publicized its new policy—"That policy is the maintenance of the principles of the Republican party, the defense of liberty, law and public morals, and the up-building of the city and county of Los Angeles and the State of South California."[76] One of the factors that allowed Otis to adopt such a stance was the population influx to Los Angeles that began around 1900, the result of a successful advertising campaign by the chamber of commerce. By 1910, thirty thousand new individuals were arriving each winter, aided by weekly excursion trains from all parts of the country. These trains brought so many to the city that the city council protested the "homemaker excursion" ads in midwestern and eastern newspapers. This strategy to limit the influx didn't work. The result was creation of a highly competitive labor market that allowed employers to keep wages low and impose their own working conditions. "From 1890 to 1910, wages were from twenty to thirty, and in some categories, even forty per cent lower than in San Francisco. It was precisely this margin that enabled Los Angeles to grow as an industrial center ... For the system to work, however, the labor market had to remain unorganized; otherwise it would become impossible to exploit the home seeker element. The system required—it absolutely demanded—a non-union open shop setup."[77]

The battle for open-shop policies began in earnest in Los Angeles in 1910, when the city's first chartered labor union, the Los Angeles Typographical Union (LATU), threatened the publisher of the *Los Angeles Times*. This union, labeled the "backbone of the city's labor movement through the turn of the century," was aggressive and persistent, turning initial verbal agreements into ironclad wage and work-shift demands. The union demanded

[76] Gottlieb, *Thinking Big,* 31.

[77] McWilliams, Southern *California An Island on the Land,*.277.

that publisher General Otis hire only union employees and pay its determined scale. Early in the twentieth century, Otis agreed, along with other local papers, to abide by these initial agreements, but as the financial condition of the *Times* improved, Otis refused further wage demands by the LATU, fired all union workers, and hired nonunion pressmen to put out the paper. "The open-shop is as simple as A B C ... It means the right of every man to control his own affairs in his own way. It means independent manhood for every willing worker in the city," declared Otis.[78]

The bombing of the *Times* building on October 1, 1910, which killed twenty people, seemed to implicate Typographical Union perpetrators, but investigation revealed that the bombers were actually members of the International Association of Bridge and Structural Iron Workers rather than the International Typographical Union (ITU). The ITU would later eschew violence as a philosophy and union tactic. James and John McNamara, along with two anarchists, were arrested and convicted and sent to San Quentin. Both McNamara brothers confessed to the crime in hopes of receiving lesser sentences. This strategy removed the death penalty but otherwise did not make a difference in the sentences—James received life in prison and John received fifteen years.

> The events beginning with the *Times* bombing and culminating in the McNamara confessions and the Socialist defeat were to affect Los Angeles labor for years to come. The immediate and perhaps inevitable result was a trying period of readjustment, of declining membership, of waning vitality. More important than these setbacks, however, was nullification of a possible victory for labor in the great struggle of 1910–1911 ... Then

---

[78]   Stevens, *Radical LA: From Coxey's Army to the Watts Riots,* 66.

suddenly, in December, 1911, the McNamaras pleaded guilty and a few days later Socialist-labor aspirations for control of the city administration were defeated. This climax sounded the death knell of both the unionizing campaign and the hope of raising labor to equality with management in collective bargaining. Thus through the *Times* bombing and related events local labor lost its clearest opportunity to vanquish the open shop. From labor's point of view it was extremely unfortunate that promised victory and expansion were defeated by forces outside the local labor movement—forces consciously identified with violence. The supremacy of the open-shop principle in industrial relations was to give Los Angeles one of its most distinctive characteristics far into the future.[79]

Other employers followed the newspaper owner's pugnacious example of fighting organized labor by refusing to hire union employees and setting their own wages, benefits, and working conditions. These companies gained support from ultra-conservative organizations such as the Merchants and Manufacturers' Association, the Better America Federation, and the chamber of commerce. Henry E. Huntington became a strong open-shop employer with his ownership of Pacific Electric and Los Angeles Railway.

The combative approach and conservative business solidarity created by the *Times* bombing and General Otis's refusal to deal with the organized labor movement would create contentious labor–capital relationships in future Los Angeles. Strikes and threats of strikes continued and often were brutally put down

---

[79] Stimpson, *Rise of the Labor Movement in Los Angeles,* 420.

by armed guards, police, sheriffs, militia, and federal troops. On his return to Los Angeles in June 1919, Harold Ferguson was confronted with both a railway strike by workers for the Los Angeles and Pacific Electric railways and threats from a syndicalist union—the International Workers of the World.

Industrial unrest would continue to exist in postwar Los Angeles. Even though workers in manufacturing jobs had increased their earnings during the war, cost of living continued to escalate. Some workers had been able to manage with the addition of overtime and bonus payments from the government, but at the end of the war, these ended, and workers were back to losing ground to inflation. "Although labor had achieved advances during the war, a major cause of industrial unrest was the feeling among many workers that, in contrast to the capitalists, they had not received what they were entitled to as a result of their wartime sacrifices."[80]

International Workers of the World on the West Coast

The American Federation of Labor (AFL), led by Samuel Gompers since 1886, had become America's trade union. Its philosophy was to form craft unions or guilds, each made up of skilled craftsmen in each labor industry. The power of this union began to erode as skilled craftsmen in mass-production industries such as steel and automobiles were replaced by unskilled non-AFL workers. The AFL, whose members had a more elitist view of themselves, tended to ignore unskilled workers, thus eroding both AFL membership and the influence of labor affairs. Other political parties and labor unions would step up to include these workers.

---

[80] Philip S. Foner, *History of the Labor Movement in the United States: Postwar Struggles 1918-1920 (International Publishers Company, Inc., 1988),*3.

By 1905 the IWW, its members often called "Wobblies," was enlisting migrant farmworkers, unskilled factory workers, black workers, Mexican immigrants, and Chinese and Japanese workers who had been excluded from other unions. The goal was "to put the working class in possession of the economic power, the means of life, in control of the machinery of production and distribution, without regard to capitalist masters."[81]

> The most exciting new phenomenon in the labor movement in the first decade of the twentieth century—the most impressionable early years of the future Communists—was syndicalism. It arose in the Western states where the craft unionism of the A.F. of L. could not or would not penetrate. The original impulse came from the Western Federation of Miners, formed in 1893. William D. (Big Bill) Haywood became its secretary-treasurer in 1901. The mine federation, an industrial union, had stormed out of the A.F. of L., charging lack of support, and had retaliated by setting up independent Western Labor centers, first the Western Labor Union, then the American Labor Union. Finally, a conglomeration of anti-A.F. of L. elements, including those in the American Labor Union, the Socialist Labor party, and the Socialist party, met together to form the Industrial Workers of the World at Chicago in 1905.[82]

A *Times* editorial by publisher Harrison Otis in 1911 aroused a strong and violent protest against the Wobblies, whose headquarters in San Diego put them in a vulnerable position with the establishment in that city: "the plain citizens of every country

---

81   Foner, *History of the Labor Movement,* 119.

82   Foner, *History of the Labor Movement,*120.

will form a combine. Its object will be the suppression of sedition and anarchy in the persons of the professional agitators … The first thing the Plain Citizens Combine will accomplish is the Quiet Removal of these gentlemen. They won't be blown up; they will just quietly disappear from human ken. With the itch removed the great disease of unrest will soon be cured."[83]

This editorial led to a revolt against the union by the San Diego power structure. San Diego was already on edge after the bombing of the *Times* when it was revealed that a radical union was responsible. The free-speech demands made by the IWW thus became a threat to the city, and after the Merchants and Manufacturers' Association (M&M) and Otis spoke to a business group in the city, the city council passed an anti–free speech ordinance. This then triggered a free-speech protest parade by a combination of the IWW, the Socialist Party, and the AFL, which violated the ordinance. The *Times* then editorialized, "The 'I Won't Workers' have organized a Free Speech league. They are against anything free except labor but they are against work in all conditions. If they went in for more action and less gab, they might come nearer realizing the satisfaction that lies in a full dinner pail."[84]

The situation quickly escalated as San Diego police, urged on by private business owners, and numerous vigilante groups combined to arrest and beat the protesters. The jails became overcrowded, and the protesters were treated harshly, but they continued to protest. Vigilante groups continued to tar and feather the protesters on the outskirts of town, but more protesters continued to invade the city.

On April 20, 1919, Governor William Stephens and the California legislature passed the California Criminal Syndicalism Act,

---

[83]   Gottlieb, *Thinking Big,* 108.

[84]   Gottlieb, *Thinking Big,*109.

aimed at violent and deadly strikes connected with IWW activities. This act made it a felony, punishable by one to fourteen years in prison, to belong to a group that advocated violent overthrow of industrial organizations.[85]

Although their presence in San Diego would end, the Wobblies continued to protest in many other cities over the next decade, attempting to win support for their radical unionism. Their chief strategy was to dispatch large numbers of lapel button–wearing, card-carrying members to designated sites, demanding that law enforcement arrest all those present under the syndicalism law. This action overloaded jails and detention centers, which became holding centers without adequate sanitary, sleeping, or eating facilities. In spite of arrests, jailing, deprivation, and physical abuse, the unionists refused to be intimidated or back down. To the contrary, groups of badge-wearing Wobblies in overloaded jail cells could be heard singing uplifting songs of solidarity!

In July 1917, General Otis's influence in Los Angeles died with him when he had a massive heart attack in his home at the age of eighty years. Although his personal combativeness ended, his spirit lived on in his newspaper, which was taken over by his son-in-law Harry Chandler, who would make him proud with his staunch support and expansion of the open shop. Less combative and aggressive, with an understated personal style, Chandler exerted much influence on the city through shrewd deal-making and a network of powerful friends.

Chandler was allied with the M&M and the chamber of commerce, both conservative groups. These men were strongly anti-union and anti-reformist and wanted to form a dedicated community of fellow believers to keep Los Angeles free of outside threats to the status quo. Thus, they formed the Commercial Federation,

---

[85]   Gottlieb, *Thinking Big*,185-201.

whose stated goal was to eliminate "trade-unionism" from the city.[86] Their target was subsequently refined to be trade unionists and left-wing radicals, which included labor unions, communists, socialists, and reformists of all stripes. Later this group became known as the Better America Federation (BAF), which would become one of the most aggressive right-wing political groups in Los Angeles.

Harry E. Haldeman, the first BAF president, was quoted as promising to bring his campaign into "every home in the county," also stating that the BAF would "kill—socially, politically and economically" any and all opponents.[87] Haldeman further goes on to state…"Its purpose is to sound a cry of warning whenever it detects the presence and influence of the radical-socialist in the government, the church, the workshop, the home. These institutions must all be protected and kept pure from the taint of radicalism; for they are the institutions to which is entrusted the duty of making better Americans."[88]

The *Times* under Chandler continued to report on the activities of the IWW. In early October 1919, the newspaper published accounts of the violent nature of the group in Los Angeles, leading the LAPD to arrest members of the group at a local gathering hall under authority of the Criminal Syndicalism Act. LAPD chief George Home promised that all IWW members would be driven out of Los Angeles. "The time has come to strike and the whole force of the police and the district attorney will be used to combat the working of the Reds who are attempting to gain a foothold in this city." The American Legion of Los Angeles organized a subset of its members to meet with DA Woolwine,

---

[86]   Stevens, *Radical LA,*167.

[87]   Stevens, *Radical LA*, 167.

[88]   Gottlieb and Wolt, *Thinking Big,* p. 190.

Mayor Meredith Snyder, Chief of Police Home, and sheriffs, who deputized legionnaires to help with law enforcement. Buron Fitts, who would later be elected district attorney for Los Angeles County, was at the time a leader in the California branch of the Legion and was appointed special district attorney.[89]

The IWW would soon become embroiled in a lethal confrontation in Washington State that killed four American legionnaires.

The Armistice Day Riot and the American Legion

> November 12, 1919—"Four American Legion men killed by IWW at Centralia, Washington."

> November 13, 1919—"Mass meeting of Los Angeles Post American Legion at Trinity Auditorium. Jack and I went. Splendid enthusiasm in organizing an emergency organization to fight IWWs."

> November 14, 1919—"Had meeting of Hollywood Post Am Legion and formed intelligence bureau of whole post to assist authorities in running down IWWs."

Harold Ferguson would be introduced to radical unionism when the IWW violently defended itself from attack in Centralia, Washington, in November 1919. The Wobblies had been active in this city since 1916, when a vigilante group destroyed their meeting hall and physically removed several members to the outskirts of the city and warned them not to return. In the spring of 1918, the group returned to the city and opened up another meeting hall in defiance of the locals' warnings. They continued to advocate for free speech in the streets of the city. During a Red Cross parade, a group of businessmen captured several

---

[89] Fitts would be elected district attorney of Los Angeles in 1928 after then DA Asa Keyes was indicted for bribery in connection with the C.C. Julian Petroleum scandal.

Wobblies, beat them, and dumped them in a ditch outside of town, repeating the warning to never return. The Wobblies' meeting hall was again destroyed. A blind newspaper salesman who sold the *Seattle Union Record* newspaper and the *IWW Industrial Worker* was likewise beaten and harassed by the anti-Wobbly forces.

But the IWW showed no signs of backing down or of being intimidated, opening a third hall in September 1919. The union's attorney advised the group members that they had every right to protect themselves and their property. The state governor and chief of police both declined to offer protection to the IWW members during the upcoming parade celebrating the one-year anniversary of the WWI armistice. The union then circulated a warning to the local citizens: [90]

To the Citizens of Centralia

We Must Appeal!

To the law abiding citizens of Centralia and the working class in general. We beg of you to read and carefully consider the following:

The profiteering class of Centralia has of late been waving the flag of our country in an endeavor to incite the lawless element of our city to raid our hall and club us out of town. For this purpose they have inspired editorials in the *Hub*, falsely and viciously attacking the IWW, hoping to gain public approval for such revolting criminality. Those profiteers are holding numerous secret meetings to that end, and covertly inciting returned servicemen to do their bidding.

One of the pillars of the American Legion when it was formed was the commitment to "protect our country from foes from within and demonstrate a virile 100% Americanism." The actions by the IWW became an offense to the Legion, and the anniversary of the armistice that had brought the war to an end was a strong

---

[90]   Foner, *History of the Labor Movement in the United States,* 214-225.

reminder of what the ex-servicemen felt they had fought for. Local employers representing lumber companies, the railroad, and the chamber of commerce had met in secret to form a Citizens Protective League with a goal similar to the Legion's—to confront and once and for all eliminate the IWW from their city.[91]

At two o'clock in the afternoon of November 12, 1919, the armistice anniversary parade began with the American Legion in the lead. The leaders of the parade chose a parade route that passed the IWW meeting hall twice. On the second pass several men broke from the parade group and entered the hall. Having expected some conflict, members of the IWW had armed themselves and stationed several of their men inside the IWW hall and in buildings across the street.[92] In the ensuing melee, four legionnaires were shot and killed, including Warren O. Grimm, the commander of the local American Legion post. The remaining men pursued the Wobblies, one of whom, Wesley Everest, was an armed ex-serviceman. Everest ran to a nearby river to escape, but instead a standoff occurred. Refusing to drop his weapon and unwilling to surrender to the mob, Everest shot and killed one of the pursuers. Everest was captured and dragged to the local jail, where he resided until that evening, when a vigilante group kidnapped him, castrated him, hung him from a railroad trestle, and shot him numerous times.

For the next several nights, teams of legionnaires combed the countryside looking for Wobblies, but only one nonunion man was found and was killed by mistake. Eventually, all but one of the Wobblies who had defended the IWW hall were identified, arrested under the Criminal Syndicalism Act, and jailed.

---

[91]   Foner, *History of the Labor Movement in the United States*, 219.

[92]   Foner, History of the Labor Movement in the United States, 219.

Except for a very few radical publications, newspapers around the country portrayed the killings of the legionnaires as an outrage perpetrated by the IWW. "It was not murder. It was an attack on the American government ... It is rebellion ... It is treason ... It was an attack on American sentiment, American honor, American tradition of right and wrong; American ideals of freedom, democracy and fair dealing."[93]

Eleven IWW members were indicted and charged with the murder of Warren Grimm. The trial, held in a highly charged atmosphere and presided over by a judge who was extremely biased, found all the indicted individuals guilty as charged, and the judge handed down the maximum sentence of twenty-five to fifty years in prison. Later attempts by the defendants' lawyers to review and appeal the sentences before the state supreme court were defeated because this court fully supported the behavior of the earlier court. By 1933 most of the parties had been released on parole.

By 1920, the Los Angeles Police Department, in response to numerous confrontations with the IWW, had established an undercover "anarchist and bomb squad" to control impending violence by radicals in LA. This squad was the precursor of the "Red Squad" in operation in the city in the 1920s and its closely related organization, the "Spy Squad," in operation in the 1930s. Both terms were used to identify this metropolitan investigation squad, which would monitor unions, political groups, and citizens whose political views were at odds with the administration, law enforcement, and conservative business groups in the city.

But the threats posed by the IWW to the structure of Los Angeles government and economy would continue for the next ten years. This group was financially strapped and had fewer members,

---

[93]   Foner, *History of the Labor Movement in the United States*, 219.

but it continued to threaten the institutions of Los Angeles. The Wobblies' strategy of acting and fighting as a unified group rather than as individuals seemed to be the most effective. Whenever the police raided one of their meeting halls to arrest members, all the attendees demanded that all in the hall be arrested since they all carried membership cards and wore IWW badges and were in violation of the syndicalism law. This tied up the jails in the city with hundreds of detainees, who slept on the floor, ate the jail slop, and urinated and defecated into slop buckets. These detainees also ended up in court and were convicted, although their convictions were overturned on appeal in many cases.

The Wobblies showed up during the San Pedro/Los Angeles port strikes in 1921 and tried to enlist union sailors and longshoremen who had been excluded from holding jobs on ocean schooners carrying lumber up and down the coast. Employers at the port had successfully excluded the San Francisco union (Sailors Union of the Pacific) that had threatened employers who did not hire union seamen and longshoremen. When the Wobblies rented and organized a hall as their headquarters in San Pedro, they became the focus of both the Los Angeles police and the Ku Klux Klan, who in a strange association assisted the police in raiding IWW halls and attacking groups of badge-wearing Wobblies.

The influence of the IWW continued to decline into the 1920s as arrests and attacks reduced its power. Its leaders would be invited by the Third Comintern in Moscow to join with the communist movement, but the IWW never agreed to this association since the organization had always had an economic target, and leaders feared that under communism the union would be taken over by politics. The union would have a second life in the 1930s as part of the Congress of Industrial Organizations, or CIO.

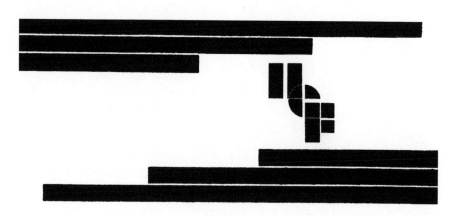

Chapter 9

The Red Scare

Socialism and American communism were political philosophies that offered solutions to unmet workers' rights that had appeared to be ignored by the open-shop business culture.

Socialism began as a utopian ideal at the end of the nineteenth century, after the publication of Edward Bellamy's utopian book *Looking Backward*, and was popular with a growing group of supporters, including literati and professionals who became known as Nationalists. Nationalist Clubs, one of which was run by socialist Henry Gaylord Wilshire, began to form around the city of Los Angeles. They met to discuss populist issues such as public ownership of utilities and railroads and ballot reform. Because the meetings were both erudite and well mannered, such forums seemed both acceptable and of interest to the general public.[94]

One individual who reflected both Progressivism and socialism (some felt these two movements were related), Christian

---

[94] Kevin Starr, *Inventing the Dream: California through the Progressive Era* (New York: Oxford University Press, 1985) *208.*

Socialist and physician John Randolph Haynes, the "father of direct legislation," became a successful advocate for city charter reform, passing referendum, initiative, and recall provisions in the Los Angeles charter in 1902 and in California in 1911. He was also a strong advocate of public ownership of utilities.[95] Progressivism succeeded in reforming municipal government in some important ways, mitigating the power and control of the Southern Pacific railroad and making "good government" a key watchword. "But what happened to the hopes of the Progressives? The War killed them ... killed many times over by the War, the Draft Act, the Versailles Peace, and the decadence that followed."[96]

Socialism offered a more worker-friendly solution to the open-shop culture of Los Angeles society. But in 1911, following the 1910 *Times* bombing, the future of socialism in Los Angeles would be dealt a severe blow. Job Harriman, who was probably the most successful socialist politician in the movement and who had worked with organized labor and politics, was running for mayor in a runoff campaign in Los Angeles against good-government (goo-goo) mayor George Alexander (an established Progressive), after having won the primary election. Unfortunately, after McNamara defense attorney Clarence Darrow made public the McNamara brothers' confession to the bombing, Harriman's popularity and chances to be elected collapsed, sounding what would be the death knell of the Socialist Party.

---

[95]   Tom Sitton, *John Randolph Haynes: California Progressive* (Stanford, California: Stanford University Press, 1992) 141.

[96]   John Chamberlain, *Farewell to Reform: The Rise, Life and Decay of the Progressive Mind in America,* (New York: The John Day Company, 1932).78.

Frank Tannenbaum, an IWW convert, wrote a warning in 1921 about socialism in his book *The Labor Movement:*

> The Socialist Party differs from other political organizations in that it concerns itself consciously about those things that *seem* to be most vital to the worker's life and labor. By its agitation it helps to crystallize discontent, gives it meaning and sets for it a definite goal. It must, however, be noted that the Socialist Party concerns itself *about* those problems *rather than with them.* It tends to postpone immediate activity by centering interest in things outside the sphere of daily contact and functions in which the worker operates, and *thus in a measurable degree* unconsciously *participates in the work performed by all other agencies that go to distract the worker's attention from this immediate problem.*[97]

The Socialist Party now faced a new challenge. Once the prospect of electoral and popular success for socialist candidates appeared unlikely, the path to the future was uncertain. Socialist Eugene Debs' attempt at electoral office in 1912 won him lots of votes (over 800,000) but resulted in defeat. Harriman saw the writing on the wall and refused to collaborate with either organized labor or political parties after this, adopting a Marxist Communist belief system advocating the overthrow of the capitalist system.

Right-wing socialists continued to work with organized labor, hoping for a political solution. However, the Socialist Party was never able to fully connect with labor or "broaden its appeal

---

[97]   Warren I. Susman., *Culture as History: The Transformation of American Society in the Twentieth Century* (New York: Pantheon Books, 1973) 76.

beyond the working-class areas of the city. At its peak, the party barely commanded 40 percent of the vote. On the rare occasions when the party won elections it hardly inspired confidence among the voters."[98]

"It is vital to the history of socialism in America to realize that the very years that witnessed the growth of considerable interest in and support for socialist ideas and the Socialist Party itself were the years that saw as well the development of 'Americanism' as an ideology, especially the first few decades of the twentieth century."[99] Americanism became one of the pillars of the newly formed American Legion, which set its sights on socialists and communists, who in the minds of Legion members were un-American and thus threats to the culture they had fought to protect and preserve.

"Not until the Russian Revolution of 1917 did a specifically Russian Communist influence make itself felt in California. Lenin was a mere name which had appeared so infrequently in the American Socialist press that scarcely a handful of non-Russians would have been able to identify him."[100] The Russian Revolution thus provided the left-wing branch of the Socialist Party a direction to the future, through partnership with the Bolshevik communists.

"On February 15, 1917 in what would be known as the October Revolution, Nicholas II, Czar of All the Russians, hastily abdicated. Six days later, he and his family were seized and imprisoned and eventually ruthlessly murdered. The three-hundred-year rule of the Romanovs evaporated in a matter

---

[98]   Stevens, *Radical L.A.*, 109-110.

[99]   Susman *Culture as History*, 77.

[100]   Susman, *Culture as History,* 72-73.

of hours. A provisional government of ten Liberals and one Socialist took over." [101]

After the Russian Revolution in 1917, Comrade Lenin accused the Allies of a secret imperialistic plot to overthrow his government. He claimed to be in possession of Czarist documents verifying his claim which he intended to publish. He demanded the Allies provide explanations for what they wished to accomplish in a victory over the Central Powers. President Wilson, along with David Lloyd George of Britain, with the assistance of Wilson advisor Edward House and a group of academics referred to later as "The Inquiry," formulated a series of proposals that they hoped would assist in peace discussions following the war. These proposals became known as "The Fourteen Points." Wilson also hoped these ideas would help bring an end to the war.

Following is a brief summary of the points:

"(1) open covenants of peace, openly arrived at, after which there would be no private understandings; (2) absolute freedom of navigation on the seas; (3) removal of all economic barriers and the establishment of an equality of trade conditions; (4) adequate guarantees that national armaments would be reduced; (5) a free, open-minded, and absolutely impartial adjustment of all colonial claims; (6) the evacuation of all Russian territory; (7) agreement that Belgium must be evacuated and restored without any attempt to limit the sovereignty that she enjoyed; (8) all French territory should be freed and the invaded portions restored; (9) a readjustment of the frontiers of Italy should be effected along clearly recognizable lines of nationality; (10) the peoples of Austria-Hungary, whose place among nations should be safeguarded and assured, should be accorded the freest opportunity of autonomous development;

---

[101] Theodore Draper, *the Roots of American Communism* (Chicago: Ivan R. Dee, Inc., 1957), *85.*

(11) Romania, Serbia, and Montenegro should be evacuated and Serbia accorded free and secure access to the sea, and the relations of the several Balkan states to one another should be determined by friendly counsel along historically established lines; (12) the Turkish portions of the present Ottoman Empire should be assured a secure sovereignty; (13) an independent Polish state should be erected; and (14) a general association of nations must be formed for the purpose of affording mutual guarantees of political independence and territorial integrity to great and small states alike."[102]

Although Harold Ferguson never addressed the Red Scare in his diary, there were many indicators that Russian influence in California was real and was a threat to local government. Reports of Bolsheviks coming to America had raised strong concerns among legionnaires during the formation of the American Legion policy planks for their new organization. One of the founding pillars of the American Legion had been to protect America from "foes from without."

Indications of developing Bolshevik Russian influence in postwar Southern California activated both the American Legion and local law enforcement to monitor and possibly detain individuals under the Criminal Syndicalism Act, should they be found to be fomenting discord. Los Angeles mayor Meredith Snyder and the Los Angeles police, county law enforcement, and American Legion combined to monitor "red" activities. The Red Squad would resort to taping conversations by "suspicious characters," which often included honest citizens expressing dissatisfaction with the ruling order. This overly broad approach, which netted more innocent citizens than hardened revolutionaries, eventually led to the disbanding of these units.

---

[102] Margaret Macmillan, *Paris 1919: Six Months that Changed the World* (New York: Random House), *495-496.*

"The American Communist Movement struggled for survival during the 1920s. By the end of the decade the Communist Party, USA, claimed a national membership of only 7545. In Los Angeles, most Communist Party members worked in the city's garment industry. Nearly all were Jewish immigrants from Russia and Eastern Europe who had moved to Southern California by way of New York City. Most lived in Boyle Heights a neighborhood located on the east side of Los Angeles."[103] Many were members of the International Ladies Garment Workers Union. "During the first two decades of the twentieth century, this union grew to be one of the most powerful in the AFL ... After the Russian revolution, many of the union's leaders and rank-and-file members left the Socialist Party and joined the communists."[104] Although communism would create a sense of fear and loathing among the American Legion and law enforcement, it never provided much of a threat to open-shop business in Los Angeles.

When Harold Ferguson returned to Los Angeles in 1919, union activities were in evidence with strikes, work slowdowns, and protests in downtown Los Angeles. Henry Huntington, who owned the railroads, refused to knuckle under and continued to run his railroad with nonunion employees. Ferguson circumvented this labor action by use of his new automobile, arriving at his workplace in the county counsel's office without interruption. He began to set his sights on outside opportunities in the real estate business, especially in the growing San Fernando Valley.

---

[103] Errol Wayne Stevens, *Radical L.A: From Coxey's Army to the Watts Riots, 1894-1965* (Norman Oklahoma: University of Oklahoma Press, 2009), 175.

[104] Stevens, *Radical LA,* 177.

Artillery Regiment insignia, Ferguson Family Collection.

Post card, "I have arrived safely overseas" August 28, 1918. Harold G. Ferguson. Ferguson Family Collection.

Captain Harold G. Ferguson, 1918, Ferguson Family Collection

General John J. Pershing, AEF, Library of Congress.

Captain Harold G. Ferguson and officers. Ferguson back row, 4th from Right. Ferguson Family Collection.

Colonel Faneuff, Commanding Officer 143rd Regiment, France 1918. Ferguson Family Collection.

143rd FA Regiment troop movement - Postcard Le Mans, France. Ferguson Family Collection.

143rd FA Regiment troop movement – Postcard Tours, France. Ferguson Family Collection.

143rd FA Regiment troop movement - Postcard
Poitiers, France. Ferguson Family Collection.

143rd FA Regiment troop movement - Postcard Poitiers
Chateau de Boivre, France. Ferguson Family Collection.

143rd FA Regiment troop movement - Postcard Bordeaux, waterfront, France. Ferguson Family Collection.

Postcard Bordeaux, France, Hotel de Ville.
Ferguson Family Collection.

Le Maréchal français Foch, commandant en chef les armées alliés

Marshall Foch, Commander of the Allied Forces,
France. Ferguson Family Collection.

World War I Victory Medal, France – The Great War for Civilization
with Army Service Clasp – given for noncombat service with
the army during World War I. Each clash inscribed with name of
country where service performed. Ferguson Family Collection.

AMERICAN EXPEDITIONARY FORCES
OFFICE OF THE COMMANDER-IN-CHIEF

TO DEPARTING OFFICERS OF THE A.E.F.

After honorably serving your
Country in a great war, you are
about to embark for the homeland.
Remember that the bearing of their
officers is reflected in the behavior and discipline of the men
you are commanding homeward bound.
I most sincerely trust that no
single act may occur to stain the
splendid record won by our troops
in Europe. My confidence and best
wishes follow you and them as you
cross the sea and in your future
service in the Army or elsewhere.

John J Pershing.

Letter to Departing Officers from General
Pershing. Ferguson Family Collection.

WINDSOR CASTLE.

Soldiers of the United States, the people of the British Isles welcome you on your way to take your stand beside the armies of many Nations now fighting in the Old World the great battle for human freedom.

The Allies will gain new heart & spirit in your company.

I wish that I could shake the hand of each one of you & bid you God speed on your mission.

George R.I.

April 1918.

A MESSAGE TO YOU FROM
HIS MAJESTY KING GEORGE Vth.

Mrs. Dolores L. Ferguson
1822 North Vermont Ave
Los Angeles, California
U. S. A.

Thank you from King George Windsor Castle,
April 1918. Ferguson Family Collection.

Program of Entertainment

given by

The 143ᵈ Field Artillery

in honor of

Mary Pickford

Saturday November 16ᵗʰ 1918.

1. Introduction.
   143ᵈ F. A. Regimental Band

2. Review of 143ᵈ Field Artillery at
   Camp Kearny by Colonel Pickford

3. A Study in Black and White.
   Groenke and Maylon, Hdqts Co.

4. Guitar Solo.
   Avilas Bat. A.

5. The Camouflage Detail.
   Mann and Stevenson Bat. C.

6. Violin and Guitar.
   Brown and Warr E Bat.

7. Piano Solo.
   Rutland Bat. D.

8. Quartette.
   Supply Co.

9. Songs.
   Taylor Bat. B.

10. "Our Mary".
    Colonel Faneuf.

11. "Farewell to my Boys".
    Colonel Mary.

12. Postlude.
    143ᵈ F. A. Regimental Band.

Last Musical Program by 143ʳᵈ Field Artillery in
honor of Mary Pickford November 16, 1918 in
France. Ferguson Family Collection.

127

33 PARIS. — Le Pont Alexandre III vers les Invalides.
Alexandre III Bridge towards the « Invalides ». — LL.

Postcard of Paris, France, Versailles Armistice.
Ferguson Family Collection.

"I am willing, no matter what my personal fortunes
may be, to play for the verdict of mankind."

President Woodrow Wilson, 1919. Library of Congress.

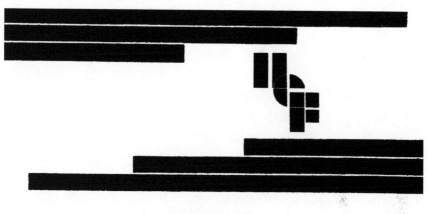

Chapter 10

Hollywood and Lankershim Ranch

Land sales and town site developments in Southern California skyrocketed in the period leading up to World War I. Prompted by railroad and chamber of commerce publicity, undeveloped, uninhabited land beckoned. Real estate speculators created new subdivisions which became the starting point for new communities. Many of these developments were interspersed between neighboring farm lands - outside of the inner city of Los Angeles - since young families wanted to raise children in nonindustrial locations as close to nature as possible. Elderly retirees came wanting to live in warm comfortable climates. Land promoters were ubiquitous at train and bus stations signing up tourists for trips to new suburbs where they could build or buy new homes. The promoters saw these newcomers as their ticked to wealth and fortune. The period between 1921 and 1928 would become the greatest property growth period in the history of the city.

The Fergusons Move to Hollywood

Harold Ferguson's family became residents of the city of Hollywood early in its development. His parents, Peter and Lillian Prest Ferguson, both citizens of Canada, moved to America in 1887, shortly after their marriage in Winnipeg. Their move was likely possible due to the railroad rate wars that reduced the price of rail tickets to ridiculously low levels, and they lived for seven years in Riverside, California. Peter was a licensed attorney and counselor-at-law in San Bernardino. Shortly after their arrival, both parents started the process of obtaining US citizenship papers, which they received in 1892. Harold would not receive his US citizenship until April 21, 1943.

Peter Ferguson's brother Alexander, also an attorney, served as Queen's Councillor for the prime minister of Canada, Sir John Macdonald, from 1867 to 1873 and 1878 o 1891. Alexander died suddenly when he was thrown from his horse, and since he had no children, he left Peter the bulk of his substantial estate.

Harold had two younger siblings—Warren and Dorothy Ferguson.

In 1895 Peter and Lillian moved to Los Angeles, where they built a home at 2324 Thompson Street. They subsequently moved to Hollywood, where they built a home at 679 Hollywood Boulevard, at the corner of Hollywood and Orange. Later the home was moved to Prospect Avenue because Harold's mother was bothered by the street noise on Hollywood Boulevard. While they were settling in, Hollywood was becoming a significant subsection of Los Angeles for prominent land developers.

At the beginning of the twentieth century, Moses Sherman, a streetcar owner and friend of both Harry Chandler of the *Times* and Henry Huntington, was building streetcar routes throughout greater Los Angeles. He devised a plan to run a line to a rural area in the northwest region of Los Angeles, and after he struck a deal with real estate agent Hobart Whitley, who had formed the Los Angeles Pacific Boulevard and Development Company, work began.

But the two men found that they needed additional capital and political connections to acquire home sites. They added Harry Chandler, *Times* publisher Otis, and bankers Herman Hellman, O. T. Johnson, and Judge Bicknell to the group, forming one of the first real estate syndicates in Los Angeles. The advantages of real estate syndicates soon became apparent—working capital, land acquisition clout, and publicity for forthcoming projects.[105] These syndicates would become exceedingly remunerative to the few individuals who became part of them.

To advertise the new town sites, the syndicate offered parts of each site at much-reduced prices to encourage buyers and ferried potential customers to sites where bands, picnics, and promoters greeted them. "Sold" signs were hung on partially finished buildings. They even built a hotel in the center of the site that became known as the Hotel Hollywood, in reference to holly berry bushes in the area.

> While the movie industry settled in, Chandler's land holdings in the Hollywood area increased. Through several dummy or family-related companies such as Chandis Securities and the Clark and Sherman Land Company, as well as through his Trust number S-5975 held by the Title Insurance and Trust Company, Chandler picked up sizeable amounts of agricultural land

---

[105] Gottlieb, *Thinking Big, 145-6*

throughout the area. His subdivisions aided in the expansion of the existing town site to the north and west of the original site. Chandler also developed economic ties to the growing movie industry, leasing buildings which later became studio properties and providing loans and investment capital for productions.[106]

Hollywood became Peter and Lillian Ferguson's home. Peter died in 1918, and toward the end of 1919, Lillian moved to Laguna Beach, where she opened one of the first pottery kilns in Laguna Beach, a developing art colony.

> December 7, 1919—"Mother's [Lillian Prest Ferguson] furniture taken by express men for Laguna."

> January 18, 1920—"Went in car with Dot to Laguna Beach to visit mother. 63 miles from our house in Hollywood to her place."

Harold married Dolores Gordon (affectionately known as Dot in his diary) in Riverside in June 1915. They adopted a daughter, Nona. When Harold returned to Hollywood after the armistice, he and Dolores rented a house at 1438 North Las Palmas Avenue in Hollywood, south of Sunset and directly below the future site of Grauman's Theatre. Harold managed the sale of two of Peter's homes and along with his sister Dorothy managed his father's sizable estate.

> June 26, 1919—"Thursday. Warm. Rented flat at 1438 Los Palmas and moved furniture from storage house to flat. Very queer to see the old familiar pieces come out of packing that I have not seen for two years. Some I had forgotten entirely. Much sport in fixing up new place. Rent

---

[106] Gottlieb, *Thinking Big,* 147.

runs from this date $40 no water payment to make. My prospects worry me."

June 29, 1919—"Sunday. Warm. Remained at house all day fixing house and working. Dolores in her element now and in best humor since I have been home. Outlined amount of furniture needed to flat which means outlay of about $400. House is going to be very comfortable when finally straightened out and new furniture moved in."

August 30, 1919—"Met and interviewed Judge Hervey of LA Trust and Savings Bank about settlement of will [Peter Ferguson's]. He insists upon bank obtaining their share. Can see fallacy of allowing bank to handle one's estate or be party thereto. They want it all."

August 31, 1919—"In evening went for walk with Dot to Whitley Hill [named after real estate developer of Hollywood] where we enjoyed a view for which that place is well known. Cannot realize beauty of Hollywood unless use such a place."

While working as a lawyer in the county counsel's office, Harold Ferguson saw an opportunity to invest in a growing real estate market in the San Fernando Valley. Jack McDowell, a friend, had bought a small well-managed farm in the same area, with lots of productive fruit trees. This triggered Harold's interest in a similar farm with walnut and apricot trees on Sherman Way in Lankershim. He was able to purchase the farm for $4,750 in September 1919. Two months later, he put the property up for sale for $7,000.

July 30, 1919—"Jack [McDowell] came over after dinner and took us both to San Fernando Valley where we bought apricots and visited Jack's ranch. His place is in splendid shape and very productive 30 acres."

September 1, 1919—"Investigated acreage for sale on Sherman Way. Hope to be able to secure a good buy in

Fernando Valley as I believe same is going to increase in value."

September 2, 1919—"Made inquiries about acreage in San Fernando Valley $5500 price quoted. Good buy at $5000."

September 4, 1919—"Requested farm advisor to make analysis of soil of Lankershim land."

September 10, 1919—"Made offer to Lee [Ken, real estate agent] on San Fernando land."

September 11, 1919—"Lee called and gave me price on San Fernando land of $4750. Will take it at that figure as I am sure it can be sold for more."

September 16, 1919—"Lee called and delivered agreements of sale and certificate of title."

September 17, 1919—"Closed deal and paid $1500 on land in San Fernando. Also ordered water connections made by LA City Water Dept. Water to be on land in week."

September 21, 1919—"Went to San Fernando in Gordon's [Hugh Gordon of University Club] Reo [Ransom E. Olds motorcar]. Made inspection of my land and placed marker for water main from Sherman Way to land for gate."

October 12, 1919—"Read and studied and in afternoon drove out to my ranch at Lankershim. Mr. Lathrop made proposition to rent on cash basis for 1/4 crops and would take care of trees at same time.

October 26, 1919—"Went to San Fernando Valley and saw Mr. Lathrop. Went over my ranch with him and agreed to give him rental of same for 1/4 crops. He will take care of trees. 21 rows across 31 rows in length. Some of trees in excellent shape and will have some apricots from them next year."

October 31, 1919—"Told Jack ranch for sale $7000."

The history of agricultural development of the valley was complicated. Two individuals, Isaac Lankershim and Newton Van Nuys, played pivotal roles in this evolution. Born in Nuremberg, Bavaria, Isaac Lankershim left home in 1836 and moved to St. Louis, Missouri, where he went to work in the grain and livestock shipping business. By 1854, he had moved to Napa Valley, where he successfully planted and harvested wheat. His wheat-growing business thrived, and by 1868, he had bought a bigger ranch in San Diego, where he continued cultivating his wheat crop.

Lankershim, along with other German-Jewish immigrants to California, bought 60,000 acres of Rancho Ex-Mission San Fernando land from Pio Pico in 1869 for $115,000. What became the San Fernando Farm Homestead Association, which included Levi Strauss of blue-jean fame, split the region in half, giving the southern half to Lankershim and Van Nuys. The two men raised sheep and grew wheat but returned exclusively to wheat farming when wool prices fell.

Isaac Lankershim's son, James Boone Lankershim, and Isaac's future son-in-law, Isaac Newton Van Nuys, took over management of the property by 1873. Van Nuys leased land from the association and using the "dryland" farming technique pioneered in the Midwest, he successfully created the world's largest wheat-growing empire.[107] This new association became the Los Angeles Farming and Milling Company.

After Isaac Lankershim died in 1882, son-in-law Van Nuys and son James Lankershim became co-owners of the vast

---

[107] Kevin Roderick, *The San Fernando Valley: America's Suburb* (Los Angeles: Los Angeles Times Books, 2001), 1-27.

property. They subdivided a large eastern area of the property and built the town of Toluca. The town changed its name to Lankershim in 1898. Van Nuys and Lankershim found this area to be better for tree cultivation since it had a shallower water table and better soil, so they sold parcels of forty acres to vineyards and to peach, apple, and apricot farmers.

In 1910 Van Nuys wanted to sell his share so that he could build a hotel in Los Angeles. The syndicate including Harry Chandler, General Otis, Hobart Whitley (who had been instrumental in the development of Hollywood), and Moses Sherman agreed to buy the 47,500 acres for $2.5 million. "The biggest land transaction ever recorded in Los Angeles County was consummated by a single lawyer, Henry W. O'Melveny, and announced in a huge story on the front page of the *Times,* on September 24, 1909." [108] Now renamed the Los Angeles Suburban Homes Company, the company wanted to provide new homeowners a chance to buy land in a desirable location close to Los Angeles at a reasonable price. By 1913, Moses Sherman, owner of the Pacific Electric trolley line, had developed a "red car" line to the Valley from downtown Los Angeles. The twenty-nine-mile trip took eighty minutes, but settlers seemed eager to view the country and were willing to take the ride.

Owens Valley Water

In the meantime, the Owens Valley aqueduct was finished amid great hopes for a bright future with this new much-needed water source but with much controversy among those who felt Los Angeles had sacrificed the Owens Valley for the

---

[108] Roderick, *San Fernando Valley,* 48.

sake of an expanding LA.[109] The terminus of the aqueduct in the San Fernando Valley didn't mean its water would be available for the valley. Federal regulations restricted delivery of water exclusively to the city of Los Angeles, so for the valley to receive additional water, it would have to incorporate with Los Angeles. On March 29, 1915, in a vote of 681 for and 25 against, the San Fernando Valley voted for its 170 square miles to incorporate with the city of Los Angeles, thus opening the region to aqueduct water and allowing the whole valley to thrive. "Annexation, as the price of water, was the means of building Greater Los Angeles," wrote historian Vincent Ostrom. Water created growth, which in turn required additional water.[110] Lankershim, which was near Hollywood and Universal City, was eventually renamed North Hollywood.

---

[109] Catherine Mulholland, *William Mulholland and the* Rise *of Los Angeles* (Berkeley, Los Angeles: University of California Press, 2000).

[110] Gottlieb, *Thinking Big,* 140.

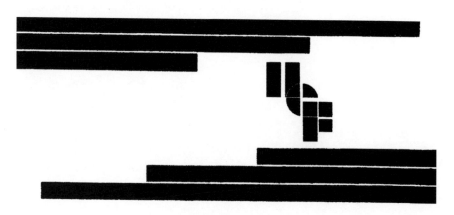

Chapter 11

Angel City Boom of the 1920s

Returning soldier Major Harold Ferguson would find LA in a growth and development spurt, a boom. Between 1920 and 1930, two million people visited or moved to Southern California, mostly from the Midwest and Mexico—brought to the city by dreams of better health and employment opportunities in a year-round Mediterranean climate.

Advertising campaigns to promote Los Angeles began in 1888, when the chamber of commerce developed a coordinated advertising effort to demonstrate the benefits of the city of Los Angeles to the nation. With colorful brochures, maps, and photos and a "California on Wheels" train to disseminate these materials, the virtues of the city were introduced to the South and Midwest. By 1920–21, the chamber had begun a promotional campaign for the "white spot" of America: Los Angeles. Photographs and postcards highlighted LA's sunny beaches with bathing-suit pinup girls. In 1921, at the suggestion of a local subscriber to the *Times*, an "All-Year Club" was instituted, advertising summer as a salubrious time to visit the West Coast. Along with newspaper and magazine ads, tourism during the summer in LA skyrocketed, and many decided to remain permanently.

Developments in transportation, coupled with real estate syndicates that put suburbs on the map, encouraged many to buy homes and put down roots. Because new residents preferred owning their own homes to renting, as was the case in other cities in America, "home-seekers" flooded the market. Increased housing created vast urban sprawl.

New prospects for tourists and new inhabitants of the city were fueled by the discovery of millions of barrels of oil, which was good for infrastructure, manufacturing, and automobiles and which also brought in millions to the economy from exports. But ocean export required a deep-water port to handle the large freighters, and in 1912 the Port of San Pedro was born, becoming the nation's second-busiest port and the first stop on the West Coast once the Panama Canal was opened in 1914.

The Los Angeles Railway, built and owned by Henry E. Huntington in collaboration with Harry Chandler of the *Los Angeles Times* and General Moses Sherman (developer of Sherman Oaks), provided transportation for visitors to LA suburbs, where subdivisions with streets, electricity, and water were promoted as new areas where tourists could buy homes.

By the early 1920s, the automobile had become a major source of urban and transcontinental transportation. Lines of early autos traveled the highways to the outskirts of LA, where encampments sprung up, populated by poor immigrants. Their camps would become new suburbs. Wealthy tourists by the millions also came for the sunshine, beaches, and undeveloped land. Henry Ford's assembly lines completely fabricated the new autos at the rate of ten per hour, thereby

The American Legion Hall Post 43, referred to as the Hollywood Legion Stadium, was constructed on El Central and Hollywood Boulevard in 1919 promoting boxing matches which attracted Hollywood luminaries and legionnaires. Clark Gable, Gene Autry, Mickey Rooney, Ronald Reagan, and Charlton Heston attended supporting the American Legion. The Olympic Auditorium (now called the Grand Olympic Auditorium) was built in 1924 on South Grand Avenue in Los Angeles. The 1932 Summer Olympic committee supported the development of the facility which separately promoted boxing and wrestling matches for decades until it was taken over by the Korean Church.

Nightlife in restaurants was busy, and theaters with live shows and movies were well attended despite Prohibition (the Volstead Act), which severely limited availability of alcoholic beverages. And of course, there were plenty of speakeasies where bootleg liquor could be imbibed if a patron knew the password for entry.

Architectural Digest magazine began publication in 1920, and with the developing technology of photography, it was able to advertise spectacular home design and decoration, as well as professional indoor and outdoor gardens, to a wide audience. The new science of landscape architecture was now available to the general public, enhancing their properties.

Numerous infrastructure projects were built in this period. Los Angeles City Hall was built, and in 1928 the Los Angeles City Council chose an empty wheat field to build the Los Angeles International Airport. In the 1920s the Hollywood Residential Complex was created by Harry Chandler, publisher of the *Los Angeles Times*, and its iconic sign announcing "Hollywoodland," which would eventually be shortened to the present-day "Hollywood," was installed on the hillside.

The general public in 1920s Los Angeles exhibited boundless exuberance in investing in manufacturing stocks, oil leases, and land in an effort to participate in the new postwar economy—instant wealth was the aim. It was suggested that purchasing Liberty bonds during the war had given rank-and-file Americans a taste of what investing could accomplish, and they wanted more. Americans took advantage of easy credit and high-spending lifestyles as the stock market continued to rise, and some economists predicted a new "high plateau" in the market. With the dark clouds of war in the past, residents and visitors to Los Angeles basked in a new optimism about their futures. "In the early 'twenties it was estimated that 125,000 visitors were spending $300,000,000 a year in Southern California."[117] Naturally, not all individuals bought into this strategy, but many did, and mindless speculation became the watchword of the decade.

> The American people, chides economist John Kenneth Galbraith "display[ed] an inordinate desire to get rich quickly with a minimum of effort." No one engineered this speculation or led investors to the slaughter, writes Galbraith. It was "the product of free choice and decisions by hundreds of thousands of individuals ... impelled to it by the seminal lunacy which has always seized people who are seized in turn by the notion that they can become very rich."[118]

Contributing to this freewheeling spending were developments in mass marketing, advertising promotions, and seemingly risk-free land sales. Stocks in American businesses along

---

[117]   Findley, *The Economic Boom of the Twenties in Los Angeles,* 242.

[118]   Jules Tygiel, *The Great Los Angeles Swindle: Oil, Stocks, and Scandal during the Roaring Twenties* (Berkeley, Los Angeles: University of California Press, 1994),8-9.

with leases on newly discovered oil in Southern California seemed to offer unending profits to investors. Salesmen were everywhere, using high-pressure, slick techniques at land and property sales events to encourage newly arrived tourists to buy a piece of land or oil leases for their future. Many new property owners resold their land for significant profit within a short period of time. New and highly successful ad techniques, including posters with shiny photographs and mailed brochures, created immediate excitement. Full-page newspaper photo-ads were also very effective in encouraging sales

Daily and tabloid newspapers and a new communication technology—the radio—opened the public to expanded information about the city and its offerings. The automobile revolutionized transportation, leading to a public that could move around the city more easily and engage socially with others. Mass-marketing campaigns involving wide dissemination of leaflets and brochures using addressograph and other machines were designed to lure retirees with cash and other migrants to mining and real estate promotions.

> No commentator captured Los Angeles in the 1920s better than Albert Atwood, who wrote a series of articles about the city for the *Saturday Evening Post* in 1923. Los Angeles alternately bemused, shocked, astounded, and awed Atwood with its vibrant energy, shameless boosterism, astonishing growth, and speculative excesses. In an article entitled "Money from Everywhere" Atwood commented on the "extraordinary and almost unprecedented pouring of population, money and prosperity into one section of the country, and more particularly into one city [Los Angeles]."[119]

---

[119] Tygiel, *The Great Los Angeles Swindle,* 12.

"Many have blamed the infusion of new money and inexperienced investors for the excessive speculation of the 1920s."[120] Secretary of the Treasury Andrew Mellon increased take-home income for the wealthy in 1921 by convincing Congress to reduce wartime excess profits taxes, lower corporate taxes, and reduce maximum personal income taxes from 65 percent to 32 percent, with the hope that the rich would have more money to invest in industry and commerce. The theory was one of "trickle-down" supply-side economics, where additional moneys at the top supposedly would raise the standards of all, but most of the new wealth never reached the target populations.

With the influx of an expanding population, new residents were in desperate need of housing. This demand triggered a powerful real estate boom beginning in the postwar period which reached its peak between 1921 and 1923. The real estate boom was likened by some to an uncontrolled speculative urge which resembled similar rampant spending in other investment arenas. Building permits rose from $28,000,000 in 1919 to $60,000,000 in 1920, $121,000,000 in 1922 and $200,000,000 in 1923. [121]

"In two years, fourteen hundred new tracts were opened in Los Angeles County and the real-estate-broker and civil-engineer elements numbered themselves in the thousands. Salesmanship became a fine art. College professor lectured on overcoming sales resistance. Preachers promoted. Each morning brokers' salesmen would gather in innumerable places for pep talks, mental shots-in-the-arm that would send them out tingling and leave them rag-weak by night. Rows of tiny

---

[120] Tygiel, *The Great Los Angeles Swindle,*10.

[121] W.W. Robinson., "The Southern California Real Estate Boom of the Twenties", The Quarterly Society of Southern California. *Vol. 24 No. 1* (March 1942) 25-30.

flags waving before every piece of acreage gave southern California a red, yellow and gala appearance."[122] The real estate boom that started in 1921 reached its peak in 1924 and slowly declined until the start of the Great Depression, when the market for new real estate ended.

The most speculative investments in this time were purchases of oil leases in newly discovered oil-rich regions. Many investors made high-percentage returns when their leases were found to be in an area containing deep pockets of oil. Standard Oil Company struck oil in Huntington Beach in 1920. Five months later, Royal Dutch Shell struck a major oil reserve on Signal Hill near Long Beach. Union Oil undertook drilling in Santa Fe Springs, which turned out to be the largest find of the three. But many investors lost all their hard-earned dollars when their leases turned out to be dry or when their trusted oil merchants turned out to be frauds and cheats. Investors in the C. C. Julian Petroleum Company were defrauded of millions, and Asa Keyes, district attorney at the time, was convicted of taking bribes from "Julian Pete" and was sent to San Quentin.[123]

---

[122] W.W. Robinson, "The Southern California Real Estate": 25-30.

[123] Tygiel, *The Great Los Angeles Swindle, 262-70.*

Captain Ferguson's promotion to Major, October 18, 1918. Ferguson Family Collection.

Major Ferguson, 1919 part of the American Relief
Administration. Ferguson Family Collection.

Herbert Hoover, Director American Relief
Administration, Library of Congress.

Hotel de Crillon,

P A R I S.

February 6th,1919.

Special Orders)
No.28   )

1.   Pursuant to authority vested in Herbert Hoover,
U.S.Food Administrator by telegraphic instructions, General
Headquarters, American E.F.,dated January 5th,1919, the
following named officers and men under paragraph three
hereof, are directed to proceed immediately to Trieste,Italy.
reporting thereat to the Official in charge of the U.S.Food
Administration and from that point elsewhere as may be
directed by the U.S.Food Administration and upon completion
of such duty to return to their proper station.

2.   It being impracticable to provide for the
expense of such travel as may be undertaken under such
orders in the ordinary course, such expense will be
provided by the U.S.Food Administration.

3.   Major Harold G. Ferguson F.A.

~~Captain Thomas M.C.Gregory, F.A.~~

Sergeant Oliver H Cash (1638734)

Sergeant George R Oliver (1638865)

BY AUTHORITY HERBERT HOOVER:

James S.McKNIGHT,
Major of Infantry,
Executive Officer.

OFFICIAL

Herbert Hoover Jan 5, 1919 ordered Major Ferguson to
report to Trieste, Italy. Ferguson Family Collection.

The UNITED STATES of AMERICA

UNITED STATES
FOOD ADMINISTRATION

TO ALL TO WHOM THESE PRESENTS SHALL COME, GREETING:

The bearer hereof ___HAROLD G. FERGUSON___

a citizen of the United States, whose photograph is affixed hereto, is traveling in behalf of the United States Food Administration for the sole purpose of food relief.

I therefore request that he be permitted to pass freely, with all property under his control, and that there be extended to him all friendly aid, protection and information which may forward the purposes of his Mission.

IN TESTIMONY WHEREOF, I, Herbert Hoover, United States Food Administrator, have hereunto set my hand this ___fourth___

day of ___February___ *, 191 9 .*

Herbert Hoover

Signature of Bearer

Travelling Pass to Major Ferguson February 4, 1919 to travel freely, from Herbert Hoover. Ferguson Family Collection.

AMERICAN RELIEF ADMINISTRATION

This is to certify that the bearer of this card
__Major Harold G. FERGUSON__ is a representative of the
American Delegation of the Interallied Food Commission.

__Il portatore di questo è constatato d'essere un
rappresentante della Delegazione Americana della Com-
missione Interalleata per l'Approvvigionamento.__

TRIESTE, __2 6 APR 1919__ _1919._

ARA ID card to Major Ferguson as American Delegate,
26 Apr. 1919. Ferguson Family Collection.

Food Relief Poster #1, 1917. Eat More Corn, Eat Less
Meat. US Food Administration. Library of Congress.

Food Relief Poster #2, 1917, America's Food
Pledge 20 million tons. Library of Congress.

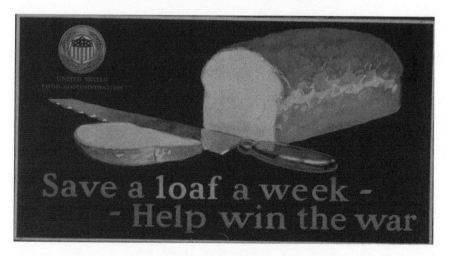

Food Relief Poster #3, 1917, Save a loaf a week,
help win the war. Library of Congress.

Food Relief Poster #4, 1917, Food will win
the war. Library of Congress

Postcard Trieste, Italy Harbor, pre-1918, FFC

Postcard Trieste, Italy La Piazza Grande. FFC

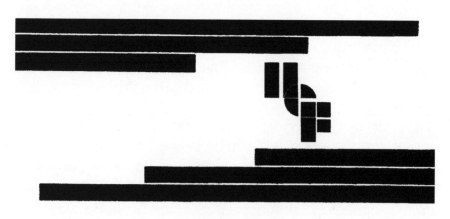

Chapter 12

Harold G. Ferguson Corporation, 1924–31

Harold Ferguson continued working in the county counsel's office until late 1920, when he left to join the California Trust Company, a subsidiary of the California Bank of Los Angeles, becoming its first trust officer. He had been thinking about a way to help small investors like himself form a business and monetary connection with larger investors interested in large monetary gains. By devising syndicate trusts, participating trusts, and other vehicles, he offered to the exuberant new investors in the 1920s a way to do well financially by piggybacking on the big-money individuals. These "syndicate trusts" would be a big part of his future.

After a year and a half, Ferguson left the California Trust Company in 1923 and joined Hugh Evans and G. C. Rhodes to form the Evans-Ferguson Company, a private real estate firm with Ferguson as vice president. The company purchased and subdivided a 285-acre tract of land in the Wilshire-Fairfax Avenues district of Los Angeles. The streets at the time were unimproved, and without any structures the landscape seemed wide open. In one particularly heavy period, the firm sold five million dollars' worth of property in nine days from a makeshift tract office. Customers often arrived in droves at the office at 6:00 a.m. to purchase tracts. The other part of the business was general brokerage and regular real estate.

Recognizing the growing investor demand for land and real estate in 1920s Los Angeles and seeking the freedom of being his own boss, he set up a full-service real estate corporation in September 1924—the Harold G. Ferguson Corporation—with initial capital of $75,000. His office in the Great Republic Life building at Eighth and Spring Streets in downtown Los Angeles was staffed by a lone stenographer.

Shortly thereafter, he formed trust number 27, capitalized at $250,000. Large beneficial interests were sold for this trust: "A beneficial interest is the right to receive benefits on assets held by another party. Most beneficial interest arrangements are in the form of trust accounts, where an individual, the beneficiary, has a vested interest in the trust's assets. The beneficiary receives income from the trust's holdings but does not own the account." Real estate was bought with these proceeds.

With this trust Ferguson intended to improve on the prior real estate syndicates used by Harry Chandler and Moses Sherman at the turn of the century. Those trusts had been limited to handpicked, wealthy, politically connected men. Instead his firm would develop and employ "participating" and beneficial-interest trusts, allowing money to be invested by all levels of net-worth individuals who wished to invest. He felt that this expanded type of real estate investing would be easier to sell to clients and more lucrative for his nascent corporation in the future.

In November 1924 a syndicate employing the name of Harold G. Ferguson Corporation negotiated a fifteen-year lease worth $300,000 to Harry and Ben Thorne, who were opening a new drugstore in the Edwards and Wildey building on the corner of Sixth and Olive in downtown Los Angeles. This area of the city promised to return significant growth.

Canoga Estates

In January 1925, four months after incorporation of his company, Ferguson—with the help of the San Fernando Corporation, an investment syndicate worth a million dollars—purchased 3,600 acres of vacant land in the San Fernando Valley between Mulholland Highway and Ventura Boulevard for $300,000. These were the last acres from the vast original Rancho holdings ceded to California from Spanish land grants. The value of the land was calculated at between $3 million and $3.5 million according to the *Examiner*. The use of this non–Ferguson Corporation syndicate was a necessity due to the expense and magnitude of the deal.

A well-known savvy investor named T. C. Brady quickly snatched up 211 acres of this land shortly after the sale to Ferguson, verifying the developmental value of the Ventura Boulevard parcel. In March 1925, the *Herald* newspaper reported that William Randolph Hearst had purchased 6,000 acres of undeveloped ranch land from Russel Brothers Ranch, located in the same vicinity. Ferguson would continue to feature Ventura Boulevard to his investors as the area of future development for the Valley, much as Wilshire Boulevard had been to Los Angeles.

The Ferguson acres, considered the largest land purchase in Los Angeles history, were wooded on rolling hillsides. Located between Mulholland Highway and Ventura Boulevard, the land parcel was to be both subdivided and developed. In ads designed for luxury home buyers, he stressed this area, which he called "Canoga Estates," as an exclusive country residential district with access to both shopping districts in Hollywood and Beverly Hills and the beach via Mulholland Drive. His plans included a 215-acre Glen Eagle Golf Club and Recreation Center Riding Club as well as a four-story class C apartment building and a Catholic church. In order for the area to have access out of the mountains, however, Los Angeles would have to complete the fifty-four-mile road.

In advertising pamphlets used to garner interest in the development, he reported that the city of Los Angeles was spending $800,000 to widen and pave streets and install ornamental lights. Small homes as well as large mansions were planned as part of this development. As of July 1, 1927, the *Times* reported one million dollars from sales of one-third of the acreage, after only a six-month period of sales activity. To further whet the appetite of potential home purchasers, Ferguson publicized a full-page glossy picture of his private $50,000 home in Canoga Estates, which he called "Galehurst," surrounded by open natural landscape in all directions. In future decades this land would be incorporated into the city of Woodland Hills.

In November 1926, the *Examiner* published information from the Ferguson Corporation on a real estate investment strategy for smaller investors. "Beneficiary interest" was part of a million-dollar Harold G. Ferguson Corporation syndicate. "Investors of small means could purchase beneficiary interest of $100 or more with $10 down and $10 per month for nine months."[124]

---

[124] "Canoga is Attracting Attention: Purchasers Show Wide Interest in Beautiful Acre Estates," Los Angeles Times, June 21, 1925, pg. G10.

Lake Arrowhead Properties

On September 3, 1925, Harold Ferguson was appointed as the sole property manager for the Lake Arrowhead Company. Lots included electricity, water, and road access. As an added incentive, boating privileges were given only to property owners. He planned to construct stables and develop bridal paths. Frank C. Platt Investment Company was appointed by Ferguson to sell the properties.

Paiute Indians had used the lake, originally known as Little Bear Lake, for their hunting grounds, but a skirmish had broken out, killing the Indians, who had set fire to a white man's cottage. Serrano Indians had come next, living peacefully with the white men while occupying Little Bear Valley for fishing and hunting. In the 1860s white men had begun logging in the area, building a lumber mill to cut the trees and haul the lumber down the mountain to San Bernardino on newly built roads.

In 1890 a reservoir to supply water to San Bernardino was planned, and the Arrowhead Reservoir Company was formed. By 1893 construction of the dam had begun. With the idea of using the water to provide hydroelectric power, a new company, the Arrowhead Reservoir and Power Company, was formed. The dam was a semi-hydraulic fill dam 200 feet in height, 720 feet long, and 1,100 feet thick.

A real estate syndicate bought Little Bear Lake in 1920 and renamed it Lake Arrowhead due to rock formations resembling an arrowhead. This had been Indian land at one time, after all. After legal delays over water distribution, the dam was finished in 1923, and a road was constructed along the north shore of the lake. The Lake Arrowhead Company syndicate saw the potential of the lake as a resort and developed the whole area. A Norman-style village complete with pavilion, restaurant, movie theater, and beach were then constructed. A nine-hole golf course and three hotels were built. Some lakeside land was subdivided and sold for private homes. Many Hollywood stars were seen staying at the hotels, and others bought homes on the lake.

On September 15, 1925, for promotional purposes, the Harold G. Ferguson (or HGF) Corporation began offering a two-day bus trip tour to the lake from the corporation's Los Angeles office for $7.50. In June 1926 a car race to Lake Arrowhead was advertised to further promote the property. Home sites from $300 to $500 and up were put on the market. In June 1926 it was reported that J. B. Van Nuys had bought a home in Arrowhead Woods. Van Nuys, who was director of the Tejon Ranch Company, was also a leader in the development of Lake Arrowhead. He was a descendant of the founding family of the San Fernando Valley, his father being Isaac Newton Van Nuys.

The HGF Corporation was growing, and so were the needs of Ferguson's business structure—in October 1925, he added the industrial and wholesale properties department, and in February 1926, he started the business properties sales department due to the corporation's determination of a "steady increase in land values" in Los Angeles. This required expansion of office space and employees.

On April 1, 1926, Ferguson was elected president of the chamber of commerce, and in the same year he became president of the University Club of Los Angeles.

In 1926 the Harold Ferguson Corporation purchased eighty acres from the Hayes Estate at Alameda and Artesia in Compton for $300,000. The parcel was purchased for a heavy industry facility due to its location adjacent to the Pacific Electric Railway, which could provide needed freight transportation.

Point Conception Land Grant

On July 24, 1927, the Harold Ferguson Corporation purchased four thousand acres of land-grant land in the Point Conception Rancho, in an area north of Santa Barbara, for $300,000. This land became part of syndicate trust number 50. With the Pacific National Bank as trustee, trust 50 had a one-million-dollar investment limit and gave the syndicate manager full discretionary power in the sale.

This purchase was made from the Rancheria del Cojo ("Cojo" being Spanish for "lame man"). Spanish explorers led by Gaspar de Portola had been the first Europeans to arrive at this coastal area in 1769, when it was populated by Chumash Indians. Jose Antonio Carrillo married Concepcion Garcia in 1809 and was granted this land as a wedding gift from Spain. The Rancho El Cojo consisted of 8,580 acres. Fred Bixby bought the Cojo Ranch in 1913 and started cattle ranching. He also bred horses, and the ranch was expanded with purchase of the neighboring Jalama Ranch in 1939. Today it is still operated as a cattle ranch and is also rented out for filming. Ferguson's idea was to develop his four-thousand-acre parcel into a seashore community.

This land-grant purchase may have come at a bad time for the corporation. In spite of favorable advertising supporting the firm's solvency and safety, 1927 was a disappointing year for the corporation. Real estate's exuberant growth and investing had begun to slow from its peak in 1924, and Ferguson's inability to sell beneficial interests in his various trusts threatened financial disaster. He opened an East Coast office of HGF Corporation on January 11, 1927, in Boston in hopes of interesting eastern investors in Los Angeles property.

Fortuitously, he met an individual who would provide a solution to maintain the company's solvency for the near future. Clayton Luckey, an executive with the Winsett Systems Corporation, offered to help sell beneficial interests in Ferguson's interests in return for 20 percent commission. This accepted offer began a game of juggling sales of properties and beneficial interests from one trust to another, showing a "false" profit that salesmen could use to encourage further sales of beneficial trusts. Under this ploy, sales improved dramatically. Luckey would join HGF Corporation as vice president of the securities department, in charge of private trusts 27, 50, 33, and 999. The new securities department for finance and syndicate operations in the HGF Corporation expanded the HGF Corporation office space by 500 percent, adding two additional floors.

Palm Ranch Antelope Valley

Harold Ferguson was soon to make another land purchase for his corporation. In September 1927 his corporation purchased two hundred acres of Western Antelope Valley land about eight miles west of Palmdale, from the old Edwin Tobias (E. T.) Earl Orchards. One of the most enticing aspects of this area for subdivision was the presence of numerous almond, Bartlett pear, and apricot trees, all of which were productive and well established. A profitable market also included the raising of turkeys. The land was being subdivided into five- and ten-acre farms. Ferguson described an abundance of water in the area. He was to name this subdivision Palm Ranch. The trustee for this syndicate trust would be Pacific National Bank. On April 1, 1928, the land offerings were open to the public.

Earl had established these lands and orchards as a result of tremendous profits he had cleared from his fruit-packing business started on a Sacramento Valley fruit ranch in 1858. It was this business of packing and shipping fruit across the country to the East Coast that would eventually help establish California as the most successful citrus-exporting state. Using the transcontinental railroad (the Atchison Topeka and Santa Fe route), the first shipment of oranges left Riverside in 1886. The following year, Earl created the Earl Fruit Company to manage the handling of oranges for transport. But there was a tendency for the fruit to freeze during cross-country transport or rot due to lack of proper ventilation in the railcars. So, Earl designed and invented a combination ventilator and refrigerator car to safeguard the fruit. He manufactured the car himself with the help of two million dollars from the Armour meat corporation, and over the next ten years his business thrived, until Armour bought him out in 1896 for $2.5 million.

With his profits Earl built a large mansion on Wilshire Boulevard at Carondelet Street and bought the *Los Angeles Express* newspaper, which he proceeded to publish. His neighbor, General Otis of the *Times*, would turn out to be very critical of Earl's progressive, good-government editorial policies. He labeled Earl "spiteful," a "fake reformer," and a "vulture." This new wealth allowed Earl to join the exclusive California Club in Los Angeles, giving him access to new networking opportunities. Harold Ferguson would later become a member of the same club and would profit from this association.

Beverly Crest Ridge Development

Long envious of the Beverly Hills area as a site for subdivision and home building, Ferguson in June 1928 was hired by a reorganized syndicate to develop a "ridge unit" in the hillsides near the Doheny Ranch. This area was called Beverly Crest, and the previous developers had already built twenty-four homes. Improvements included ornamental electric lights, underground conduits for utilities, sewers, cement streets, and Los Angeles aqueduct water. The sites had a view of Catalina Island and a "majestic panorama of the mountains, downtown Los Angeles and the Pacific."[125] Along with the homes themselves, swimming pools, gardens, and patios were added features. Prominent buyers included George Arthur, a movie star, and Al Jolson.

The Beverly Crest Syndicate was headed by Earl Gilmore, owner of Gilmore Oil Company. Major stockholders included actor, comedian, and producer of silent comedy films Harold Lloyd and stage and film actor Milton Sills. The syndicate board had recently reorganized and had added members.

On September 8, 1928, the HGF Corporation purchased a ninety-nine-year lease worth six million dollars on a property at Sunset and Vine Streets in downtown to establish a major business center. This property was acquired from Hood Lease with the help of an outside syndicate.

Hoover Dam and Imperial Valley Water

On December 20, 1929, in a full-page advertisement in the *Evening Herald* titled "Nature's Gift to Los Angeles and Southern California," the HGF Corporation, along with thirteen construction and real estate development companies, endorsed the Boulder Dam project to dam the Colorado River at Boulder City on the Nevada–Arizona border. HGF's plans for development of the Indio area had been threatened by flooding of the Colorado

---

[125] Los Angeles Times, The Harold G. Ferguson Corporation, "In Beverly Crest, the balcony of beautiful Beverly Hills" (June 2, 1928), Advertisement.

River. Indio was an important city because it was situated along the rail lines from Los Angeles to Yuma, Arizona. Its future development, as seen by HGF and others, was dependent on the construction of the dam to tame the Colorado River and bring much-needed water to the area. Upon its completion in 1936, the dam would be renamed "Hoover Dam" for Herbert Hoover, who served as secretary of commerce in the Coolidge presidency, the period when the project originated.

Due to accelerated growth in Los Angeles, Owens Valley water was projected to be insufficient for continued growth in the region. William Mulholland, superintendent of the Los Angeles Water Department, recommended using Colorado River water, which had been used for some time to irrigate land in the Imperial Valley. In 1922 a federal Colorado River Commission, chaired by Hoover, worked on an agreement eventually known as the Colorado River Compact, which was ratified by six states, including California.

After ratification of the compact, a federal Bureau of Reclamation bill was proposed to build and "operate a power generator and high-water storage facility on the Colorado River near Boulder."[126] This bill was sponsored in Congress by Philip Swing, a California representative, and Senator Hiram Johnson. The Swing-Johnson bill also provided for an "All-American Canal" to continue to bring irrigation water to the Imperial Valley.

When the Boulder Dam bill passed in Congress in December 1928, the canal amendment also passed. Construction began on the dam in 1931.[127] Eventually, Los Angeles and several other cities voted to create the Metropolitan Water District.

---

[126] Gottlieb, *Thinking Big,* 181-183

[127] Gottlieb, *Thinking Big,* 180-183

Malibu Movie Colony and Malibu La Costa

Ferguson had some big plans in the works for his corporation when some Hollywood friends requested a secluded beach property, they could use to get away from the stresses of the filmmaking business.

In 1892 Frederick and May Rindge had purchased a large parcel of land on the coast of the county of Los Angeles, land originally owned by the Chumash Indian tribe and which in time would become Malibu. Mr. Rindge, a resident of Boston who had attended Harvard for one year, had become rich when his father died, leaving him a large fortune. He had become one of the wealthiest men in America. With a family history of rheumatic fever—all of his siblings succumbed to the effects of the infection, and he himself had endured a severe case— he did not want to remain in the East after his father's death. Having heard of the healthful climate of the West Coast, he decided to move with his new wife May to Southern California, where he purchased an isolated parcel of cattle-raising country offering both him and his wife peace and solitude. Frederick was chronically ill, necessitating horse-and-buggy travel to a faith healer, Madame Emily Preston, in an isolated region eighty miles north of San Francisco, overlooking the Russian River. She applied blistering ointments and poultices designed to assuage his pain and boost his immune system. Her compound was a destination for many afflicted with illnesses, with people arriving from great distances for her healing applications. Frederick eventually built her a church in the region out of gratitude for the feelings of well-being she had instilled in him.

The beach and cattle property the Rindges purchased had a long history. Following the Chumash occupation, it had become part of a Spanish-era rancho. In 1802 Bartolo Tapia was granted a long splinter of land on the coast called Rancho Topanga Malibu Sequit. That land was purchased in 1848 by Leon Victor Prudhomme, who had married into the Tapia family, for four hundred pesos. Prudhomme was also a landowner in Southern California. The property was then resold in 1857 to Matthew Keller at ten cents an acre for 13,315 acres. He raised cattle on the land. Frederick purchased the Malibu property from Matthew's son Henry for ten dollars an acre.

Frederick and May were very protective of their land and privacy and hired security guards to evict trespassers. Access to this area was accomplished only on horseback or by horse-drawn carriage. There were no roads.

After Frederick died, May Rindge became the sole owner of the land and became very active in trying to preserve the land from access by the outside world, although there were many who wished to connect to this portion of the coast. Mrs. Rindge formed Marblehead Land Company in 1921 to manage the complex land holdings created by Frederick before his death.

The Southern Pacific railroad threatened to build a train route through the Rindge land. To counter this threat, May Rindge filed suit against the railroad and, in addition, installed railroad tracks on her land that never carried trains but blocked other railroads from access. The cost of this phantom train ran to over one million dollars and drained more of her fortune.

Many of her legal dealings to prevent outside intervention into her protected sanctuary were conducted through the law firm of O'Melveny and Myers in Los Angeles. Although these efforts were temporarily successful in postponing the inevitable, the legal bills were hefty and ate away at the remaining fortune left by her husband.

Other unexpected expenses began to appear as well. The county tax assessors had decided the land was more valuable than originally assessed, so they increased her property taxes. Also, in 1913 the Sixteenth Amendment introduced the federal personal income tax, which required her to begin paying income taxes. In 1916 the County Board of Supervisors approved taking portions of the ranch through the power of eminent domain for roads. In August 1916 her son Samuel filed a lawsuit to liquidate the estate to try to stop its dissipation by her multiple legal actions. He demanded ownership of Malibu be taken away. May offered some property on Wilshire and Fairfax to him if he would drop the legal action, which he did. She then ceased any future dealings with him.

On January 11, 1919, a state judge ordered Los Angeles County to pay May Rindge $41,000 for use of her land to build a highway. May continued to refuse use and access. In 1921 Congress ratified and President Harding signed the Federal Aid Highway Act, setting aside money to develop a national roadway system. The growth of automobile traffic had made this legislation necessary as horses and horse-drawn carriages disappeared and automobiles traveled the highways of America. May Rindge continued to obstruct plans by the county of Los Angeles to invade her private land space. In 1922 Los Angeles built the first few miles of county road from Santa Monica to Malibu, but the project was stopped by fences placed at the entrance to the Rindge estate.

In 1923 the case found its way to the Supreme Court, which disallowed further attempts to restrict road building, and by 1925, Los Angeles County had given May Rindge a check for $98,000 in compensation for land taken under eminent domain for road building. Although she desperately needed the money, she never cashed the check because she denied governmental authority to dictate her rights. But her fight over land access was finished. The road was finally opened in 1929, which completed a final piece in the road connection between Mexico and Canada. "It is a tale that could have happened only during the brief sliver of history in which the advent of railroads and the automobile meshed with the limitless American frontier and anything seemed possible."[128]

In 1926 Harold Ferguson contacted May, looking for a way to access a one-mile stretch of coast at the eastern end of the property to form a beach colony—not being adjacent to any roads meant it was a perfect sanctuary away from public access. At first she was reluctant, but she was in desperate need of money and realized that the HGF Corporation could provide money from land leases and help her pay off debts. She had requirements, however. In order to obtain the leasing rights for this property, Ferguson had to agree to sell only ten-year leases. Additionally, the agreement stipulated that at the end of each lease, the structures could be torn down, returning the land to its undeveloped natural state. Ferguson agreed, and on September 16, 1926, HGF was named the exclusive leasing representative for Malibu Ranch on 1.0 miles of beach between Las Flores Canyon and the western boundary of the ranch. Other beach property was reserved for the red clay discovered during digging, used by Malibu Potteries to make the popular and colorful Malibu Tile. Ferguson then began advertising the availability of Malibu Ranch land to the general public by placing colorful billboards that depicted families playing on the beach, emphasizing "privacy" and "tranquility."

---

[128] David K. Randall, "The Making of Malibu: How Malibu went from private paradise to Hollywood enclave," Lapham's Quarterly (March 10, 2016):1-9.

Soon after the billboards were erected, one of the most popular silent film actresses in Hollywood, Anna Q. Nilsson, contacted Ferguson and was the first to lease one of the one hundred properties. The word was out, and soon Marie Prevost, a silent film star and flapper, signed up for a lease. Many more Hollywood stars followed. Raoul Walsh, a one-eyed movie director, showed interest. Suddenly, the Malibu Colony had become the Malibu Movie Colony. Due to the uncertain future for buildings in the colony, Hollywood studio set designers were hired to build beachfront cottages. These were, by definition, flimsy structures with thin walls and foundations. During drunken arguments, inhabitants could put their fists through the wall and into their neighbor's cottage.

The general public was captivated by the glamorous, playful lifestyle of these actresses, actors, and directors. Newspapers and tabloids were full of stories and photo montages of famous people in private pursuits. Once the first tennis court was built, Mary Pickford and Charlie Chaplin would play tennis together, with candid photos of their matches receiving wide distribution and thrilling the nation.

Edgar Rice Burroughs, who successfully authored several Tarzan novels, including *Tarzan of the Apes*, bought a home at 90 Malibu La Costa Beach and in 1933 was elected honorary mayor of Malibu. He also published the Malibu Modern Age Comics, which included *Tarzan #1: Love, Lies and the Lost City Part One*. In writing his novel *Tarzan of the Apes* in 1912, he described this idyllic setting: "He longed for the little cabin and the sun-kissed sea—for the cool interior of the well-built house, and for the never-ending wonders of the many books." large ranch that Burroughs purchased in San Fernando Valley in 1919 would later become a neighborhood called Tarzana, with residents agreeing to name the community after Burroughs's hero.

May Rindge was relieved by and justified in her decision to open the land once she began receiving $660,000 per year from Movie Colony leases. All that she asked regarding all the hoopla was to be left out of any publications or photographs. This income helped to cover accumulated legal debts since her whole desire was to avoid selling off Malibu property.[129] Because of Harold's success in leasing these properties, she developed trust in and reliance on his real estate expertise for future dealings.

In 1929, May Rindge again needed money. She was building a mansion on the hillside above Malibu, and the costs were sky-high. So, she sought out Harold Ferguson and offered to sell subdivided land in the hills above Malibu, along with 7,500 feet of beachfront private property that made up the La Costa Club. Homes on the hillside land would provide panoramic ocean views as well as isolation from the hubbub of oceanfront developments. But infrastructure would be necessary to make these plots accessible. The HGF Corporation thus would have to provide concrete roads, underground electricity, electric lights, and sewers. It would even build a large reservoir to store water for use by hillside neighbors.

Homeowners would then have the right to use the beach at La Costa without restrictions, though they would have to find a way down the hillside and across the highway to the beach club. Ferguson planned to build a tunnel under the highway to make access to the beach easier, more secluded, and safer.

---

[129] Randall, "The Making of Malibu", 1-9.

The contract was for the sale and purchase of approximately 593 acres of the Malibu Ranch for $4,943,652. This purchase included 7,500 feet of ocean frontage. The down payment required of HGF Corporation was $1,000,000.

A contract between HGF Corporation and Marblehead Land Company was signed, and the Malibu Trust (number 1013 through Bank of America as trustee) was formed. Escrow opened in the fall of 1928 and closed on March 11, 1929. A deposit of $995,000 was paid to the Marblehead Land Company by Bank of America. The balance of the purchase price was to be paid in installments over a period of years. For all the money paid to the trustee or collected by Harold G. Ferguson Corporation, certificates of beneficial interests were issued at the rate of 1/2000 for each one thousand dollars subscribed and paid in.

The Trusts

During Ferguson's business lifetime, he and those he hired helped to form several trusts of various types. This summary of the trusts and their contents will help the reader to understand the next section of this story.

Trust number 27 was formed in 1928 and was run by a syndicate manager with full discretion regarding which properties were to be included. Private trust 33 was formed in 1929 with US National Bank as trustee and with a capitalization limit of five million dollars. This trust included many business properties in Los Angeles, including properties at Wilshire Boulevard and La Brea; Sunset and Vine; Wilshire Boulevard at Hamilton Drive; Hollywood Boulevard between Wilcox and Cahuenga, across from Warner Brothers Studios; North Vine Street; West Sixth

Street west of the Richfield Oil Building; and Sixth and Flower Streets.

Trust 50 was opened in 1927 and was closed June 21, 1928, with a capitalization limit of one million dollars, with the syndicate manager having uncontrolled discretionary power of sale. Pacific National Bank served as trustee. Once this trust became oversubscribed, further subscriptions were switched to trust 33.

Trust 999, which had a fifty-million-dollar limit, was formed in 1929 with US National Bank as trustee. It was formed by Harold Ferguson with authority to buy and sell real property or interests in real mixed or personal property of any kind.

Trust 1013, or the Malibu Syndicate trust, was formed by Ferguson interests in 1929 for the sale of lots in the Malibu La Costa purchase. Bank of America served as trustee for this trust.

Other syndicate purchases, as mentioned, were outside of the trusts and included Lake Arrowhead, Canoga Estates, Palm Ranch Antelope Valley, and Beverly Crest Estates.

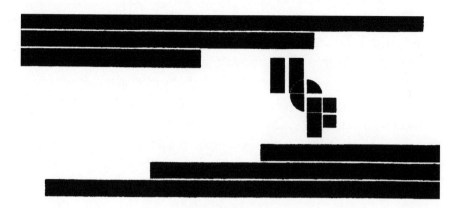

Chapter 13

Stock Market Crash and San Quentin

"'A new era and new forces have come into our economic life and our setting among nations of the world,' Herbert Hoover said in accepting the Republican presidential nomination in 1928. 'These forces demand of us constant study and effort if prosperity, peace and contentment shall be maintained.'"

> The list of changes in the generation since the close of the nineteenth century seemed endlessly amazing ... "epoch-making events" that filled the first third of the twentieth century: the Great War, mass immigration, race riots, rapid urbanization, the rise of giant industrial combines like U.S. Steel, Ford, and General Motors, new technologies like electric power, automobiles, radios, and motion pictures, novel social experiments like Prohibition, daring campaigns for birth control, a new frankness about sex, women's suffrage, the advent of mass-market advertising and consumer financing[130].

---

[130] Kennedy, *Freedom from Fear,* 11-13.

"Black Thursday," October 24, 1929, was the start of the Wall Street crash. The following Tuesday ("Black Tuesday"), October 29, was the fourth and last day of stock market decline. During the four days of the crash, the stock market fell 25 percent, which equated to more than the cost of World War I. The market hit bottom on November 13, 1929. It would not return to its pre-crash high until November 1954.

The prominent banks of the day tried to stop the crash. Morgan, Chase National, and National City Bank of New York bought shares of stock to restore confidence in the market. Their intervention produced the opposite effect since investors saw this as a sign that the banks were panicking, producing an 11 percent further drop in the market.

Over the next month the market seemed to stabilize somewhat, and many in the business and banking community in Los Angeles felt a sense of relief when the financial health of the city seemed to be returning to a more normal state. But the worst was yet to come, and despite a government response to the crisis, which no one had seen coming, the country slid into the Great Depression, which would be the worst economic downtown in US history.

The Harold G. Ferguson Corporation was not immediately affected by the stock market crash or the Depression, and the company continued to plan for a bright future in Los Angeles real estate. Ferguson himself remained a popular and trustworthy figure and was elected president of the California Stock Exchange in 1929.

He was also elected to lead the Los Angeles Realty Board in 1930. In his speech to the board in December 1929, at its annual meeting at the Biltmore Hotel in Los Angeles, he painted a rosy picture for the economy and real estate in the coming year. In attendance at the meeting were Mayor John Porter and Rufus B. von KleinSmid, the fifth president of the University of Southern California (1921–47).

After a business trip to assess the country's economic health, Ferguson was quoted in a local newspaper: "The most striking aspect of the business situation throughout the east and middle west is the fact that the sound manufacturing and mercantile concerns are going ahead with expansion plans as though nothing had occurred in the stock market, because it has had no appreciable unfavorable effect on their activities. And this means that capital and population will continue to flow to Southern California." Ferguson further stated "that large eastern reservoirs of capital are showing unprecedented interest in real estate, industrial and municipal loans in Southern California. The general public interest in the southland is widespread and intense."[131] On May 29, 1930, Ferguson purchased the Western National Bank, renaming it Central National Bank

A copy of a letter found in the Ferguson papers, written in 1930, cast doubt on the rosy predictions the HGF Corporation was making regarding the shape of its trusts. This letter refers to trust number 33:

> Dear Sir; the trustee under the trust has given notice of its resignation as such trustee but no successive trustee has as yet been named. As a result of the general business depression that has for some time existent and which continues and by reason by various attacks made upon the syndicate manager, it has been impossible to

---

[131] Hollywood Citizen News, "Ferguson Has Welcome News from East," Vol. 8, No. 261, August 31, 1929.

profitably dispose of the trust properties, with the result that the trust now has various obligations which it is unable to meet. There is now due on account of principal, taxes, interest and other expenses which are necessary or proper for the preservation, maintenance and care of said trust properties a sum approximately $280,000 which is about 10% of the face value of the trust certificates issues and subscribed for. By reason of indebtedness now due and maturing the properties of the trust are being jeopardized and unless funds are contributed by the certificate holder, or otherwise obtained, it is inevitable that serious losses will be suffered.

By January 1931, Ferguson's corporation and future would take an unexpected downturn. A new state corporation commissioner had arrived. Raymond I. Haight, who had been appointed by sitting governor James Rolph, had his sights set on corporations he felt were operating illegally. As the new corporation and banking sheriff in town, he threw down the gauntlet in the *Los Angeles Record* on January 21, 1931: "Now because of the disintegration of the fraud-investigating department [state of California, Commissioner of Corporations] no adequate check has been kept on these bankers and corporations. The result has been that the fly-by-night brokers and concerns have used the department as a cloak behind which to hide their crookedness. We are going to stop this. I expect co-operation from the district attorney of Los Angeles County [Buron Fitts] in our efforts."

Haight had attended USC's law school and entered law practice in Los Angeles in 1920, creating the firm of Haight and Mathes, which had gained a reputation for investigating corporate fraud.

After heading the state corporate commissioner's office for three years, he would enter the 1934 race for governor and lose to incumbent Frank Merriam, who had become governor after the death of James Rolph. In that race he would be advised to run as an independent since Upton Sinclair, a utopian socialist (running an End Poverty in California campaign, or EPIC), was running on the Democratic ticket. Refusing, Haight would continue to run as a Democrat, thus splitting the vote and helping to elect the more conservative Merriam.

On January 17, 1931, Haight suspended the stock and securities permits for ten Harold G. Ferguson companies, sending a letter detailing alleged "mismanagement" to District Attorney Buron Fitts for further investigation. These "companies" consisted of six companies and four trusts. The companies were H. G. Ferguson Corporation; H. G. Ferguson Building Corporation, Ltd.; Harold G. Ferguson Finance Co., Ltd.; Ferguson-Smith Co., Ltd.; Southern Sugar Company; and Ferguson-Holman Co., Ltd. The four suspended trusts were trust 999 (US National Bank as trustee), trust 33 (US National Bank as trustee), private trust 50 (Metropolitan Trust Company of California as trustee), and private trust 27 (Harold G. Ferguson as trustee). Additionally, according to Haight, trust 1013 had been operating illegally without a license.

Accusations stated that the HGF Corporation had received excessive commissions for its activities and had violated certain provisions of the corporate trusts, including illegally transferring funds from one trust to another. A few small investors with unrealistic expectations for their investments had hired lawyers and sued both HGF Corporation and Harold Ferguson personally. The new commissioner then had been forced to act to "protect the public" through his initial filings. Haight sent a letter to District Attorney Buron Fitts outlining his findings along with a recommendation for prosecution. Fitts reviewed the allegations and then conducted a long private meeting with Ferguson in his office.

The soil in the city at the time had been contaminated by other high-profile fraud cases. There had been several instances of illegal corporate behavior during this period, which may help to explain the state's aggressiveness in closing the HGF Corporation.

The first such case was the Julian Petroleum oil lease scandal of 1927, in which 40,000 investors lost $150 million. The district attorney, Asa Keyes, was convicted of bribery by the corporation commissioner and was sent to San Quentin. It was during the trial of this case that Motley Flint, a successful banker and Hollywood syndicate member, was shot and killed by one of the bankrupt investors. The Richfield Oil Company went into receivership in 1931 after a $54 million debt was found, due largely to illegal spending on personal comforts by company officers. Next, the Guaranty Building and Loan failed when its president embezzled $8 million. Finally, the American Mortgage Company failed with debts of $18 million.[132]

On February 10, 1931, Harold G. Ferguson and vice president Clayton Luckey were arraigned on a complaint originating in the district attorney's office charging them jointly with forty-eight violations of the state's Corporate Securities Act. Within two hours of the signing of the document detailing alleged manipulations of real estate and funds totally approximately $719,000, the two surrendered to the sheriff and were scheduled to appear for a preliminary hearing on March 2, 1931, at 9:45 a.m. They both were released on $10,000 bond.

---

[132] McWilliams, *Southern California an Island on the Land,* 245-6.

The preliminary hearing was set to evaluate the details and merits of the allegations—essentially a fact-finding hearing.

Many of the counts that Haight had alleged involved technical violations of state corporation laws, all pertaining to the Malibu Syndicate (trust 1013). The first twenty-six counts were complaints by individuals that Ferguson and Luckey had sold them interests in the Malibu Syndicate formed by Ferguson in March 1929 for sale of lots in Malibu La Costa without first obtaining permits from the commissioner, which Ferguson had been told by the previous commissioner he didn't need.

In Ferguson's personal corporate documents, he wrote,(direct quote)

> No permit was issued by the [previous] commissioner of corporations, State of California for the issuance or sale of certificates of beneficial interest in this trust; although advice has been given that no such permit was necessary. It is now the contention of the commissioner of corporations [Raymond Haight] that a permit was necessary for the issuance and sale of such certificates.

> A number of suits are threatened against the three banking institutions above named in the event there is a decision rendered holding these certificates to be securities and that a permit from the commissioner of corporations was necessary. These suits involve the theory that money paid to or by these banks were for void certificates and that no such expenditures should have been made by them.

> *There are several hundred trusts in the same*
> *condition in the trust departments of other banks*
> *and trust companies which might be subject to*
> *the same attack.*[133]

Count number 27 charged the two with selling interests in the Malibu holdings to trust 33 without a permit. Ferguson made these and other transfers in order to cover the $1 million down payment to buy the Malibu La Costa properties. The next charge was that a $350,000 interest was sold from trust 1013 (Malibu Syndicate) to trust 33 without a permit. Additionally, both Ferguson and Luckey were charged with four counts of making sales of Malibu property in trust 999 without a permit and with making additional sales to trusts 999, 50, and 27 without permits. It would take four to five months of extensive review of company records to reach the final conclusions on which the trial would be based.

The newspaper accounts accusing Ferguson of defrauding 17,000 investors of eight million dollars were falsely sensational and designed for shock value. The enormity of these accusations was intended to connect Ferguson to other flagrant corporate fraud cases, creating doubts among the public about the soundness of corporate leadership. These sensational amounts would be significantly reduced as the trial proceeded. The overzealous prosecution, which ruined both Ferguson's company and his business life, seems to have been an attempt to earn Haight a reputation as a tough, no-nonsense public servant who could single-handedly reform corporations, helping him in his 1934 run for public office.

---

[133] Personal letter among Ferguson Papers - "Facts Relative to Investment in Malibu Trust in Bank of America By United States National Bank and Pacific National Bank."

On July 7, 1931, both men were indicted and were sent to the Superior Court for a nonjury trial before Superior Judge B. Ray Schauer, charged with forty-one counts of conspiracy, grand theft, and violation of the California Corporate Securities Act. When the judge was questioned about the lack of a jury, he responded that with a jury the trial would be unnecessarily long, and by shortening the length of the trial, he could save money for the taxpayers. The prosecution was to be handled by Bonner Richardson, chief of the district attorney's corporation department, with help from David L'Esperance and Ray Brockman, who had spent months evaluating the evidence. A few weeks following the indictment, the United States National Bank closed its doors to prevent its customers from filing civil suits arising out of this prosecution.

The trial began September 28, 1931, and according to the press promised to be the most complicated criminal trial in Superior Court history. After four-plus months of information gathering, including expert review of the company files and records, the charges were clarified. Fifty-five witnesses were subpoenaed for the prosecution, and an unknown number were to be employed for the defense. The entire case revolved around the handling of funds in various trusts in the corporation.

During the trial the prime allegation showed that in 1927, Ferguson was having difficulty selling beneficial interests in his several trusts, threatening the firm's survival. The real estate market had begun to slow, and it had become increasingly difficult to prove to investors that dividends in their investments were robust. Clayton Luckey of the Winsett Systems Corporation had offered a unique solution, agreeing to sell beneficial interests in the trusts for a 20 percent commission. With the HGF Corporation agreement, the game of shifting sales of properties and beneficial interests from one trust to another began, allowing salesmen to demonstrate good dividend returns on a selected trust. Once investors realized that strong dividends were showing up on the balance sheets, sales in that trust began to grow, rapidly.

As soon as he took office, Luckey began reporting on the successful sale of certain trust 27 properties, allowing the trust to pay large dividends. Reports of these dividends from trust 27 were then used to sell beneficial interests in trust 50, capitalized at one million dollars. This was so successful that the trust was soon oversubscribed by a hundred thousand dollars. Trust 33 was then organized to accept these sales and was capitalized at five million dollars. Thus, the firm showed rapid growth over two years based on false dividend advertising from trust 27.

With the success of this "fake profit" scheme, Ferguson and his corporation were rescued, and Luckey became vice president of all trust sales. The commissions made on sales of beneficial interests in five HGF Corporation trusts during these transactions amounted to three million dollars, of which Ferguson received $1.7 million and Winsett Corporation received $1.3 million.

Secrecy became the watchword in relation to various trust activities. One letter to sales directors in the firm warned, "Please be advised that under no circumstances are the copies of the declaration of trust for Trust No. 33, now in your possession, to leave your office nor will any copies thereof be made. There are no exceptions to this rule, whatsoever, and any infringement whatsoever thereof will automatically sever your connection with this company. Signed—CLAYTON LUCKEY."

A large share of investors' losses came from a substantial HGF Corporation investment in one of its promoted companies—the Southern Sugar Company. In a trial statement, Ferguson explained that $400,000 of funds from trust 999 was invested in the company a short time before it collapsed. He made the investment after consulting with bankers, believing his stockholders would profit. The firm failed and was taken over by receivers.

After numerous delays in scheduling and rescheduling witnesses, the trial proceeded, and on November 17, 1931, Ferguson testified in his own defense.

> Meeting the charge of the State that he illegally used investors' funds in trusts 27 and 50 of his corporation, Ferguson said he considered the trust securities as real estate, and that with the advice of bankers he believed it not illegal to use the trust funds for real estate security.

> In defense of his asserted acts Ferguson referred to the prior success of trusts 27 and 50 which, he said, paid investors large returns, and the foundation was laid to show that real estate slumps and general depression were responsible for the failure of the corporation, rather than any act of Ferguson. The witness [Ferguson] said also that any variance in the listing of securities was made on the advice of his bankers.[134]

On December 11, following a ten-week trial, Harold G. Ferguson was found guilty on twenty-five felony counts—sixteen counts of grand theft and nine counts of securities fraud. In a nonjury trial, sitting judge Schauer who was solely responsible for the final verdict summarized his conclusions from all the days of

---

[134] FERGUSON'S STORY TOLD TO JURORS: Financier Takes Witness Stand to Defend Actions. *Los Angeles Times,* 11/17/31.

testimony: "Specific instances were cited in which the court said Ferguson's actions were not those that would be expected of a reputable member of the bar. The prosecution contends the two men 'faked profits' to boost the sale of beneficial interests in the trusts and misrepresented the nature of the trust and safety of investments therein."[135]

On December 18, defense counsel Frank Doherty and Ray Nimmo asked for a new trial on the grounds that the original trial had not provided a fair hearing and that there had been misconduct by the district attorney and the court; without a jury the entire decision about such a complicated case had been in the hands of one man—Judge Schauer. The judge's summary statement cast even more doubt on the rationale for his conclusion. Thus, it was not surprising when on the following day Ferguson and his defense team were denied a new trial, and he was refused an application for probation. Ferguson was sentenced to San Quentin for a period of "five to fifty years."

In spite of evidence uncovered during the trial implicating Luckey in the scheme to falsely portray the trusts as profitable, and despite his also having received inordinately high commissions, the creator of the "false profit" ploy was found not guilty.

The court blamed Ferguson for the seven-million-dollar loss to his investors after the state prematurely withdrew all of his permits on technicalities, ending his business and his relationship with these investors. Had he been allowed to continue his business while the investigation continued, evidence suggested that the Malibu Syndicate, which had been off to a good start, could have been successful, providing his investors with even greater returns on their money. Closing the whole thing down prematurely

---

[135] FERGUSON LEARNS HIS FATE TODAY, *LA Record, 12/11/31.*

only worsened the outcome. The court imposed this exorbitant sentence without even considering a petition for parole. This was partly due to the many angry individual investors who attended the trial, seeking Ferguson's blood and revenge for a temporary cessation of their dividends, which exerted undue influence on the outcome of the "trial."

In January 1932, Ferguson began to serve his term in the Los Angeles County Jail. On June 23, 1932, shortly before 6:00 p.m., he was transferred from the county jail to the Southern Pacific Station, loaded under guard along with eighteen others on the regular prison car, and sent to San Quentin. He was assigned number 51429.

An appellate court on August 26, 1933, upheld Ferguson's conviction but reversed one count of grand theft. A review reported theft of $65,000 from investors by illegal transfers of funds between five trusts to make a showing of false profits. "In reversing the Corporate Security Act charges [nine counts] that Ferguson had sold securities without a permit, the court ascribes error to the trial judge in refusing to allow Ferguson to attempt to prove that he had consulted the Corporation Commissioner and that he had been advised that no permit was necessary to sell interests in one of the trusts."[136]

Prosecutorial overreach had unfairly ended a successful and profitable real estate business that had involved some irregularities in 1927 but that had righted the ship and entered a new phase of growth and profit, not only to the company but also to the many investors. Up until Ferguson's pardon by Governor Merriam in December 1938, questions about these proceedings would remain.

---

[136] FERGUSON TRIAL VERDICT UPHELD, Los Angeles Times, August 26, 1933.

After Ferguson had served three years and three months of his sentence, the State Board of Prison Terms and Paroles announced he would be released from prison on parole March 23, 1935. Released on the same day was James Talbot, former president of Richfield Oil Company of California, who had served two years and four months of an eight-year sentence.

"I want to get back to work, make a living, support my family and be let alone," Ferguson was quoted as saying to his family when he returned his sister's home once he was back in Los Angeles.[137] Shortly thereafter, he reported to deputy state parole officer James E. Lewis, from whom he received instructions on his conduct over the next three years. Ferguson joined his mother Lillian, wife Nora, and daughter Betty. Until a new home could be found, he would live with his sister, Mrs. Joe Duncan Gleason, in her family's home on North Edgemont Avenue. Ferguson said he planned to start work immediately. He reported that while in prison he had done work in offices and gardens.

On December 28, 1938, a full pardon was given to Harold G. Ferguson by Governor Frank Merriam after a recommendation by the Advisory Pardon Board on December 22, 1938. "Now I, F. Merriam, Governor of the State of California, pursuant to the authority vested in me by the Constitution and Statues of said State, do hereby pardon Harold G. Ferguson, San Quentin No. 51429, of the crime of Grand Larceny; and Violation of Corporate Securities Act."

---

[137] Personal communication documented in Ferguson Family Archives.

Magazine cover, 1902, The Land of Sunshine, illustrated
by Joe Duncan Gleason. Gleason Family Collection.

Advertisement 1898, Illustrated Joe Duncan Gleason, The Home
Seeker and California Tourist. Gleason Family Collection.

Cover of Pamphlet, Sunny Southern California, Illustrated
Joe Duncan Gleason, Gleason Family Collection.

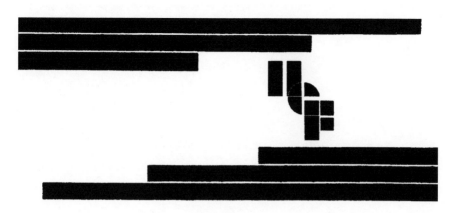

Chapter 14

Post–World War I and the Great Depression

When Major Ferguson returned home from Trieste, Italy, in 1919 after serving under Herbert Hoover in the American Relief Administration as a manager of food relief to Europe, his military days were over, and he was relieved to leave Europe and the military behind. His efforts to receive shipment of relief supplies and distribute them to designated countries facing famine had accomplished many of the goals of the program, and the participants in this endeavor were justifiably proud of their hard-fought successes.

These successes had been made possible by American farmers, who had been encouraged to increase their crop production to provide surpluses that could be shipped overseas to Belgium and later to allies Britain and France, as well as Germany, Yugoslavia, and Russia. With Hoover's encouragement, farmers had become voluntary participants in this endeavor and had put marginal lands to cultivation, increasing their crop yields dramatically. Horses and mules were replaced with gasoline-engine tractors, making cultivation of larger acres of land possible. Eighty-five thousand such tractors were purchased by individual farmers and utilized during the five-year period of the war. Since horses and mules were no longer needed, they were destroyed, opening up thirty million acres of pasture land for planting of wheat or cotton and for grazing dairy animals.

Following the armistice of November 1918, world demand for agricultural production returned to prewar levels, and American farmers found themselves with huge staple food surpluses and without the wartime markets to sell them.

> Prices plummeted. Cotton slumped from a wartime high of thirty-five cents per pound to sixteen cents in 1920. Corn sank from $1.50 per bushel to fifty-two cents. Wool slid from nearly sixty cents per pound to less than twenty cents. Although prices improved somewhat after 1921, they did not fully recover until war resumed in 1939. Farmers suffocated under their own mountainous surpluses and under the weight of the debts they had assumed to expand and to mechanize. Foreclosures increased, and more and more freeholders became tenants.[138]

The federal government under then president Calvin Coolidge tried to aid farmers by controlling commodity prices and providing funding for agricultural cooperatives, but a major bill passed by Congress, the McNary-Haugen Bill, which would have made the federal government the buyer of last resort for the farm surpluses, was twice vetoed by the president.

Herbert Hoover was elected president in 1928 and was inaugurated on March 4, 1929. Raised by a Quaker uncle, Hoover had always believed in the power of individuals over government to solve economic problems, and soon after his

---

[138] Kennedy, *Freedom from Fear,* 17.

election, he began to apply his philosophy to the country. Individualism, voluntarism, and connection to community were guiding lights promoted by the new president, who at first eschewed government intervention into the emerging economic and social problems of the country.

After the demise of the famer-relief McNary-Haugen Bill, one of the first acts by president-elect Herbert Hoover in 1929 was to sponsor and sign the Agricultural Marketing Act, designating certain corporations to buy surpluses and hold them off the market to stabilize price levels. But these corporations soon exhausted their funds as the agricultural depression of the late 1920s and early '30s expanded. Farmers would continue to struggle and would become the hardest-hit victims of this expanding depression.

Before solutions could be improvised by the president, another stumbling block would be created. Congress had already imposed high tariffs on foreign goods in 1922 under the Fordney-McCumber Tariff Act, but protectionist Republicans in Congress wanted to increase tariffs still further, particularly on agricultural imports but also on manufactured goods. A bill known as the Smoot-Hawley Tariff Act of 1930 imposed the highest import tariffs in American history. Many economists and advisors pleaded with the president to veto this legislation, but he saw some pluses to the bill and lacked the political will to confront a determined Congress. The imposition of these tariffs would put a damper on American foreign trade with countries that had also erected tariffs.

As the growing depression threatened urban America, Hoover searched for non–federal government interventions to rescue the economy. He was able to report some success in dealings with the Federal Reserve System. The Fed had lowered its discount rates to member banks, easing money supply, and also agreed to refuse discounts to banks that had made stock market call loans. In a meeting with several top industrialists, Hoover suggested that companies voluntarily maintain wages at their current rate rather than reduce wages, which he projected would help to maintain public optimism. The majority agreed to this suggestion. Easing access to money and maintaining wages, though small steps, seemed to offer hope. In addition, Hoover resorted to federal intervention and in three years nearly doubled federal public works funding.

By April 1930 the market had regained ground from its earlier fall, and the banking system seemed stable. In a speech to the chamber of commerce on May 1, 1930, Hoover remarked, "I am convinced we have passed the worst and with continued effort we shall rapidly recover."[139] Most Americans believed that this downturn was one of the self-limited business-cycle downswings that had existed over decades and drew hope from Hoover's remarks. Yet the economy continued to slide.

Failure of the American Banking System

The banking sector, closely tied to agriculture, was poorly organized, managed, and funded and would soon show signs of collapse. As 1930 came to an end, a series of bank failures cast doubt on further recovery. American banking had not been on solid footing even with a good economy. Throughout the 1920s, banks had failed at a rate of five hundred per year. In the last two months of 1930, an additional six hundred banks closed their doors. The incredible number of banks that had been operating in the country, all as individual businesses unconnected to governmental safeguards or oversight,

---

[139] Kennedy, *Freedom from Fear,* 58.

contributed to the cause of these closings. Many small banks were seriously undercapitalized. Had branch banking been in operation, smaller banks could have depended on their larger parent urban banks to support them when investors demanded withdrawals of their money. But because of the Populist revolt in the late nineteenth century, this remedy was not available for smaller banks, and therefore they had to close their doors. Even the smaller number of banks that were members of the Federal Reserve System fared no better since the Fed did not undertake corrective action to keep them open.

In November 1930 disaster hit Louisville's National Bank of Kentucky, and collapse

> then spread virulently to groups of affiliated banks in neighboring Indiana, Illinois, Missouri and eventually Iowa, Arkansas and North Carolina. Mobs of shouting depositors shouldered up to tellers' windows to withdraw their savings. The banks, in turn, scrambled to preserve their liquidity in the face of these accelerating withdrawals by calling in loans and selling assets. As the beleaguered banks desperately sought cash by throwing their bond and real estate portfolios onto the market—a market already depressed by the Crash of 1929—they further drove down the value of assets in otherwise sound institutions, putting the entire banking system in peril. This vicious cycle—a classic liquidity crisis magnified to monstrous scale in the inordinately plural and disorganized world of American banking—soon threatened to become a roaring tornado that would rip the financial heart out of the economy.[140]

---

[140] Kennedy, *Freedom from Fear,* 66-67.

By December 11, 1930, the crisis had struck New York, with the City Bank of the United States closing. Known as the "Pantspressers' Bank," this bank held the deposits of thousands of Jewish immigrants, many of whom worked in the garment trades. Even at the request of the Federal Reserve, J. P. Morgan refused to come to the aid of the failing bank, in a gesture of its anti-Semitism. This represented the largest bank failure in the country at the time and shook the country's confidence in the banking system. The failure of the Federal Reserve to save the bank also damaged the country's confidence in the Federal Reserve System.

But cautious optimism returned in early 1931, when bank failures were down and economic activity seemed to be recovering. Hoover, along with many Americans, began to hope that the country was seeing the beginning of the end of this depression. Up to this point, the depression had seemed American in nature—flagging automobile sales, a downturn in housing markets, the stock market collapse, a disorganized and weak banking system without federal controls, and most surprisingly, a collapse of a previously robust agricultural powerhouse.

But Europe was poised to insert itself again into American affairs, turning the American depression into the Great (Global) Depression and severely limiting Hoover's ability to deal with an expanding economic crisis.

In his memoirs Hoover described a deepening understanding and appreciation of the depth of this depression and its ultimate cause:

> In the large sense the primary cause of the Great Depression was the war of 1914–1918 … just as we had begun to entertain well founded hopes

that we were on our way out of the depression, our latent fears of Europe were realized in a gigantic explosion which shook the foundations of the world's economic, political and social structure. At last the malign forces arising from economic consequences of the war, the Versailles Treaty, the postwar military alliances with their double prewar armament, their frantic public works programs to meet unemployment, their unbalanced budgets and the inflations, all tore their systems asunder.[141]

This began with the electoral success of the Nazi Party in the German parliamentary elections of September 1930. This electoral success was based on the fear and anxiety of the German people as their economy declined—the result of crippling war reparations payments to allies Britain, France, and the United States. This fear had opened the door to the rising oratory of Adolf Hitler. The German Weimar chancellor, Heinrich Bruning, attempted to improve the situation by forming a customs union with Austria, but this alarmed the French, who saw this as an attempt by the Germans to annex Austria. France began tightening the money supply on Austrian banks, which led to the closure of Vienna's largest bank. A chain reaction then began, spreading through banking systems in Germany and its neighboring countries and leading to bank closures.

International debts and reparations payments since the war had become tangled and convoluted. Initially, under the Treaty of Versailles, Germany was required to pay $33 billion to cover civilian damage during the war. In 1923, France had invaded the Ruhr Valley of Germany to enforce payment by Germany, causing an international crisis and eventual implementation

---

[141] Kennedy, *Freedom from Fear,* 71.

of the Dawes Plan of 1924. This plan outlined a new payment method to help Germany meet its payment schedule, but by 1929 the Young Plan renegotiated and decreased further the amount Germany was required to pay, amended to US$26.2 billion.

Demanding little in wartime reparations from Germany, the United States had come out of World War I as a leading financial creditor. America's solid financial status was due partly to the US treasury and private banking institutions having acted as lending banks to several European countries. Britain and France owed America $10 billion in repayment of US Treasury loans taken during and after the war. Money had been loaned to Germany in the 1920s by private US banks to assist in Germany's payment of reparations to both France and Britain, who in turn applied this money to their own debts with the United States. Germany relied on continuing American loans to continue to pay the Allies, but the stock market crash of 1929 disrupted the monetary supply chain.

France was agreeable to canceling German reparations, but only if the US agreed to cancel France's debt. This outraged Americans, who saw this strategy as an attempt by Europe to pass costs of the war onto the US. Many Americans still blamed President Wilson for having agreed to enter the war in the first place. "Iron-toothed insistence on full payment of the Allied war debt thus became not only a financial issue but a political and a psychological issue as well, a totem of disgust of a corrupt Europe, a regret of having intervened in the European war, and of provincial America's determination not to be suckered by silky international financiers."[142]

In spite of the US Congress's reluctance to consider reduced Allied debt payments, on June 1, 1931, Herbert Hoover called

---

[142] Kennedy, David, *Freedom from Fear,* 71-73.

for, and Congress eventually ratified, a one-year moratorium on payment of war debts—principal and interest—for all nations. German payments were eventually canceled in 1932.

The Gold Crisis

The German banking panic and Britain's abandonment of the gold standard had significant impact on the American financial system, which was still recovering from massive bank failures. Remaining banks still had on their books German and Austrian loans of $1.5 billion, which would turn out to be worthless. American investors picked up on the fear and panic in Europe and began withdrawing gold and money from US banks. Runs on banks continued, leading to 522 bank failures in the month following Britain's going off gold, and by the end of 1931, 2,294 US banks had closed.

The Smoot-Hawley Tariff would play a major role in deepening the economic downturn. This act implementing protectionist trade policies was signed into law on June 17, 1930. It raised US tariffs on more than 20,000 imported goods. It was instituted to regulate commerce with foreign countries, to encourage the industries of the United States, and to protect American labor. The tariffs in the act were the second-highest in the US in one hundred years. Retaliatory tariffs by America's trading partners resulted in a reduction of American exports and imports by more than half during the Depression. "The passage of the Smoot-Hawley tariff exacerbated the Great Depression."[143] Although President Hoover signed the bill, in retrospect he regretted passing it and felt he had been trapped by an unfriendly Republican Congress.

---

[143] Kennedy, David, *Freedom from Fear,* 49.

The consequences of this protectionist trade barrier affected Britain, Germany, and the US by decreasing tax revenues. As a result of exorbitant tariffs on foreign trade, along with increased unemployment and industry slowdowns, governments were forced to institute tax increases on economically fragile populations in order to pay for public works and welfare services.

Up until 1931, gold had been the basis for the majority of the world's currencies. Gold had guaranteed the value of money and especially guaranteed the value of a country's currency beyond its borders in trade with other countries. Incoming gold increased money supply, and outgoing gold reduced it. Currencies were valued based on a ratio of currency in circulation to gold reserves. Incoming gold was supposed to expand the monetary base, inflate prices, and lower interest rates. Outflowing gold reduced money supply, deflating prices and raising interest rates. For a country such as Britain, which had exported much of its gold supply to European creditors and which held large remaining war debts, the lack of gold supply created an impossible situation. America was demanding that the country repay its debts, but this was becoming too expensive in view of Britain's reduced gold reserves. Therefore, on September 21, 1931, Britain defaulted on further gold payments to foreigners, thus going off the gold standard. This action was soon followed by more than twenty other countries.[144]

Germany, whose currency had become worthless, was forced to devalue its currency in 1931 during the bank panic. Japan followed Britain, going off the gold standard in December 1931.

Hoover was not in favor of abandoning the gold standard in the US, but he was not confident that his solutions to the economic abyss were working. His personal beliefs against

---

[144]   Ibid, p. 74-76.

federal government intervention to solve economic problems remained, in part because at this stage the federal government was too small to envision massive relief. He began various experiments with the economy during his remaining time in office, in a desperate attempt to stop the economic collapse.

On October 4, 1931, he met privately with several advisors, including Treasury Secretary Andrew Mellon. He urged stronger private banks to create a pool of money to help weaker institutions and tried without success to form a privately funded National Credit Association. But he soon realized that privately funded solutions for these immense problems were futile and that federal government involvement was necessary to begin to solve the economic problems. This began what became known as Hoover's "second program" against the Depression, going beyond the voluntary measures tried in the past.

The Glass-Steagall Act of February 27, 1932, marked the first time when paper currency could be allocated to the Federal Reserve System. It was an effort to arrest deflation and expand the Federal Reserve System's ability to offer loans to member banks (rediscounts) on government bonds and commercial paper. It authorized the Fed to (1) lend to five or more Federal Reserve System member banks on a group basis and (2) issue Federal Reserve Bank Notes (i.e., paper currency) backed by US government securities, when a shortage of "eligible paper" held by Federal Reserve Banks would have required such currency to be backed by gold. This act opened gold reserves in the Fed, expanding money supply.

In November 1931, Hoover proposed that Congress provide twelve new home loan banks for home-mortgage holders with a rediscounting service like the Federal Reserve System. Congress, in its usual anti-Hoover, uncooperative mood, delayed passage of the Federal Home Loan Bank Act until late 1932.

But banks needed money, and to deal with this, Hoover in 1932 created the Reconstruction Finance Corporation (RFC). Labeled as the most radical, most innovative idea under Hoover's administration, the RFC provided a way to make taxpayer dollars available to private financial institutions. Congress funded the RFC at $500 million with authority to use up to $1.5 billion. "The RFC was to use these sums to provide emergency loans to banks, building-and-loan societies, railroads, and agricultural stabilization corporations."[145]

Farming and farmers had not fared well. Crops had rotted, livestock had died, and the Federal Farm Board's stabilization corporations had exhausted their funds. There seemed to be nothing the government could do to stop the downward spiral. Unemployment soared and was increasingly prevalent in ethnic and immigrant communities. Highways and railcars became crowded with dirty, unkempt men looking for a job, any job. By early 1932 over ten million were out of work, and those who kept their jobs often ended up working part-time. Smaller paychecks or no paychecks were the rule. There had been no attempt to institute federal unemployment insurance in the past, and in the current time frame, such legislation was not on the horizon. The situation of such high unemployment with few to no social services had never been experienced in America before, and there was no adequate support for the affected individuals, who numbered in the millions.

Hoover remained wedded to his philosophy of encouraging state and local governments and private charitable groups to provide relief for the ongoing economic collapse, and as these attempts

---

[145] Kennedy, David, *Freedom from Fear,* 83-85.

failed, Hoover's popularity plummeted. In July 1932, thousands of unemployed members of the American Expeditionary Force descended on Washington. They had renamed themselves the Bonus Expeditionary Force and came to lobby Congress for early cash payment of a war service bonus that had been promised to them. Congress refused the requests, but many vets remained in the city. When DC police tried to evict them, a riot erupted, and Hoover called in federal troops led by General Douglas MacArthur, who evicted the men and burned their shacks. Two veterans were killed in the melee. This episode led to further deterioration of Hoover's reputation and his ability to effectively deal with these overwhelming national concerns, which at the time seemed beyond repair. This set the stage for the election in November 1932 of Franklin Roosevelt.

The US devalued its currency in 1933. With these currency devaluations, debts and reparations were cheaper since they could be paid in the devalued currency instead of by the transfer of gold from the country's gold deposits. Industries also became more competitive.

However, currency devaluation throughout the world introduced financial chaos and uncertainty in an already chaotic situation, leading the world to return to the gold standard in 1944 at the Bretton Woods Agreement.[146]

---

[146] Lewis, Nathan, *Was the Gold Standard the Cause of the Great Depression?* Forbes Magazine, 4/1/2012

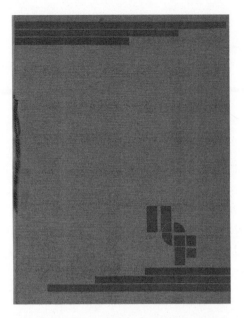

Logo, Harold G. Ferguson Corporation
Brochure. Ferguson Family Collection.

HAROLD G. FERGUSON

President of Harold G. Ferguson Corporation,
1929. Ferguson Family Collection.

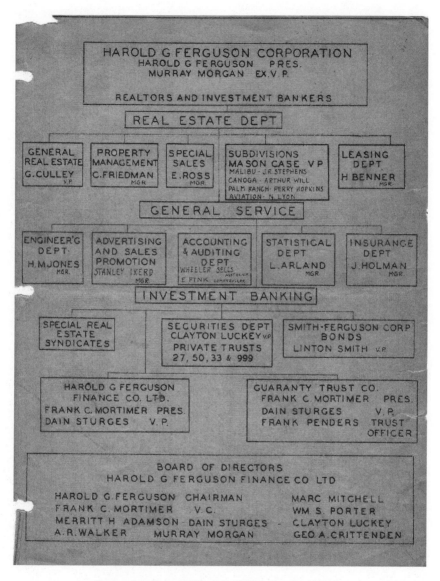

Organizational Chart, HGF Corporation,
1929. Ferguson Family Collection.

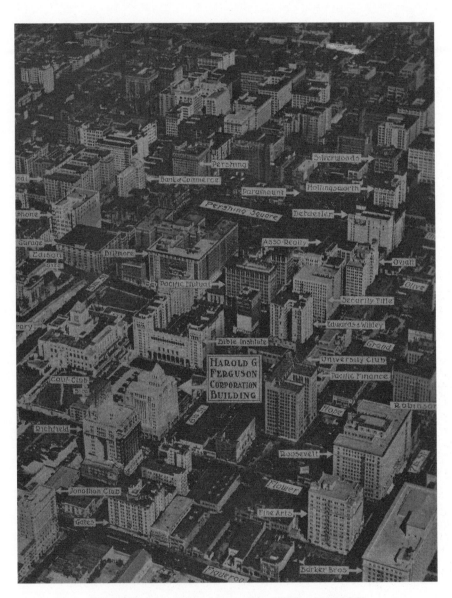

Aerial Photo of Los Angeles 1928 with HGF
Corp. Ferguson Family Collection.

Projected HGF Building, 1928. Ferguson Family Collection.

HGF Corporation Christmas Party, 1928.
Ferguson Family Collection.

Canoga Estates Field Office and Map, HGF
Corporation 1925. Ferguson Family Collection.

Canoga Estate Home of HGF, 1927. Ferguson Family Collection.

Interior Home of HGF, Canoga Estate. Ferguson Family Collection.

View of San Fernando Valley from Canoga
Estates. Ferguson Family Collection.

Harold Ferguson and actress Ruth Roland, signing lease for Malibu Movie Colony. Ferguson Family Collection.

Photo of Malibu La Costa from HGF Corp. brochure. Ferguson Family Collection.

Malibu La Costa road development. 1929.
Ferguson Family Collection.

Photo of new home at Malibu Movie Colony. Brochure
HGF Corp. Ferguson Family Collection.

Panoramic view of Antelope Valley – HGF Corp Palm
Ranch Development. Ferguson Family Collection.

Palm Ranch Advertisement of Almond Picking in Palm
Ranch. HGF Corp brochure. Ferguson Family Collection.

Completed Hoover Dam, 1936. Huntington Library
and Botanical Gardens, San Marino California.

Conclusion

By 1932, Herbert Hoover's presidency was coming to an end, and Harold G. Ferguson was incarcerated in San Quentin prison. Very different men with radically different backgrounds, both had worked to save Europe during and after the war, and both had been undone by the Great Depression and the delayed effects of the world war. Neither man would be the same after his experiences, and each would have to find a second life that would allow him to survive.

In 1937, Ferguson was given a real estate license in Nevada, and he resumed working in real estate. He continued to be active in American Legion activities and meetings. He opened a small office in Los Angeles, where his niece Eleanor worked for him. After his divorce from Dolores citing "cruelty" Ferguson remained single. On December 12, 1941, he re-married Hazel Gadbury in a Las Vegas ceremony. At the time he was living in Burbank, California. Later he purchased a small home in Covina, where he carefully tended his garden. He lived a quiet life, gardening, visiting, and spending time with his sister Dorothy and other family members, and he left many fond memories to those who knew him. In 1950, working out of a real estate office at 3723 Wilshire Boulevard, he began publicizing a parcel of land in Apple Valley, California, known as Desert Knolls, which was being developed as a new family community. The area, previously a desert, was described thusly in his brochure: "The clear bracing air, abundance of sunshine and pure water makes this an unusually healthy place to live."

He died June 25, 1963, from a sudden fatal heart attack and was buried in Hollywood Cemetery. His funeral ceremony was performed by the American Legion with many former soldiers and friends in attendance. The list of individuals who attended his funeral was impressive, and many eulogies were delivered attesting to his keen mind and his wonderful qualities of wit, humor, and kindliness. Many personal letters, from the family archives, were written by his friends testifying to his friendship and positive personal qualities. "Even the bad parts he met with understanding and added experience so in his later years found him to be such an attractive loving man with so much depth and enjoyment of life that it was a real tonic to be around him. Oh how much we will miss him." Another comment of note— "The old members of the Hollywood Post who cherish the memories and traditions of their first commander."[147]

Harold Ferguson lived and worked during a time of great growth, technological advances, and social upheaval in Los Angeles. The decade of the 1920s set in motion many trends that would eventually determine how a small agricultural village with a population of 1,600 when California joined the Union in 1850, without a port and with no natural resources, including water, would become one of the country's largest and most vibrant metropolises. Much had to be done to make this a reality, not the least of which was changing the city from primarily agricultural to industrial and urban, and this at times was a bruising process.

The early settlers who inhabited the city and made up its power structure had their own ideas about how changes should be accomplished, and the individuals and groups who made up the elite were determined to resist influences they saw as exported from other parts of the country. These men saw Los Angeles as unique—not like other metropolises. It had unique geography, climate, and habitats. But the railroads ended the city's isolation from other American regions and brought in many outside influences, which by their nature created contradiction and

---

[147] Personal letters from Ferguson Family Archives.

conflict. There were fights and struggles, but change came, industrialization happened, and urbanization was the inevitable consequence.

The main determinant of the direction and future development of the city was the immigrants who arrived in large numbers. By 1930, the city was home to two million individuals. Many of these individuals had left large urban centers where industry and living space were in proximity to one another, and they thus had strong desires to form good, wholesome communities at a distance from downtown commerce and industry. Small dispersed subdivisions were better environments in which to raise families and were safer and cleaner. These men and women envisioned single-family subdivisions surrounded by developing commercial businesses—which was a major improvement over urban centers they had left behind and offered the best hope of good communities.

Los Angeles had gone through a decade of massive transformation from its simple beginnings to a thriving metropolis, with overwhelming population increase, postwar adjustments, and financial stresses on an economy that could not mature and adjust fast enough to the new realities of globalization. Some individuals adapted and adjusted to the new Los Angeles. Others were caught in the jaws of the Wild West.

Bibliography

Books

1. Barry, John M. *The Great Influenza: The Epic Story of the Deadliest Plague in History.* Penguin Books, 2004.

2. Bellamy, Edward. *Looking Backward: 2000–1887.* Bantam Books, 1888.

3. Chamberlain, John, *Farewell to Reform: The Rise, Life and Decay of the Progressive Mind in America,* the John Day Company, New York, 1932.

4. Crosby, Alfred, *America's Forgotten Pandemic,* Cambridge University Press, 1989, 2nd edition, 2003.

5. Davenport, Matthew J., *First Over There: The Attack on Cantigny, America's First Battle of World War I,* St. Martin's Press New York, 2015.

6. Draper, Theodore, *the Roots of American Communism,* Ivan R. Dee, Inc., Publisher, Chicago, 1957.

7. Eisenhower, John S.D., *Yanks: The Epic Story of the American Army in World War I,* Simon and Schuster, Touchstone, New York, 2001.

8. Faulkner, Richard S., *Pershing's Crusaders: The American Soldier in World War I,* University Press of Kansas, 2017.

9. Findley, James Clifford, *The Economic Boom of the Twenties in Los Angeles,* PhD dissertation Claremont Graduate School, 1958

10. Finney, Guy, *Angel City in Turmoil: A Story of the Minute Men of Los Angeles in Their War on Civic Corruption, Graft and Privilege,* Amer Press, Los Angeles, 1945.

11. Fogelson, Robert, *the Fragmented Metropolis: Los Angeles 1830-1950,* University of California Press, Berkeley and Los Angeles California, 1967.

12. Foner, Philip S. *History of the Labor Movement in the United States: Postwar Struggles 1918-1920,* 1988 International Publishers Co. Inc. 1988.

13. Gottlieb, Robert and Wolt, Irene, *Thinking Big: The Story of the Los Angeles Times its Publishers, and Their Influence on Southern California,* G.P. Putnam's Sons, New York, 1977.

14. Hallas, James H. ed., *Doughboy War: The American Expeditionary Force in WWI, Stackpole Books 2009.*

15. Hutson, William Gardiner, *My Friends Call Me C.C.: The Story of Courtney Chauncey Julian,* Sunstone Press, 1990.

16. Jeansonne, Glen*, Herbert Hoover, a Life,* New American Library, Penguin Random House LLC, 2016.

17. Kennedy, David M, *Freedom from Fear: The American People in Depression and War, 1929-1945,* Oxford University Press, 1999.

18. Kennedy, David M, *Over Here: The First World War and American Society,* Oxford University Press, 1980.

19. Kolata, Gina, *Flu: The Story of the Great Influenza Pandemic of 1918 and the Search for the Virus that Caused It,* Touchstone, 1999, Epilogue 2005.

20. Larson, Erik, *Dead Wake: The Last Crossing of the Lusitania,* Crown Publishers 2015.

21. Macmillan, Margaret, *Paris 1919: Six Months That Changed the World,* Random House/New York, 2001.

22. Macmillan, Margaret, *the War that Ended Peace: The Road to 1914,* Random House/New York, 2013.

23. Manchester, William, *the Last Lion: Winston Spencer Churchill, Visions of Glory 1874-1932,* Little Brown and Company, Canada, 1983.

24. Mayo, Katherine, *That Damned Y: A Record of Overseas Service,* Houghton Mifflin Co., the Riverside Press Cambridge, 1920.

25. McWilliams, Carey, *Southern California an Island on the Land,* Gibbs M. Smith Inc., Peregrine Smith Books, Salt Lake City 1983.

26. Mulholland, Catherine, *William Mulholland and the Rise of Los Angeles,* University of California Press, 2000.

27. Nussbaum, Robert L., *Thompson and Thompson genetics in medicine* – 6th ed./Robert L. Nussbaum, Roderick R. McInnes, Huntington F. Willard, W.R. Saunders Company, 2001.

28. Price-Smith, Andrew T., *Contagion and Chaos: Disease, Ecology, and National Security in the Era of Globalization,* 2009, Massachusetts Institute of Technology.

29. Randall, David K., *the King and Queen of Malibu: the True Story of the Battle for Paradise. W.W. Norton* and Company, 2016.

30. Roderick, Kevin, *The San Fernando Valley: America's Suburb,* Los Angeles Times Books, 2001.

31. Rumer, Thomas A., *the American Legion: An Official History,* M. Evans and Company, Inc., New York, 1990.

32. Sitton, Tom. *John Randolph Haynes: California Progressive,* Stanford University Press, 1992.

33. Sitton, Tom & Deverell, W, *Metropolis in the Making: Los Angeles in the 1920s,* University of California Press, 1999.

34. Smith, Jean Edward, *Eisenhower in War and Peace,* Random House Trade Paperbacks, 2012.

35. Starr, Kevin, *Inventing the Dream: California through the Progressive Era,* Oxford University Press, 1985.

36. Starr, Kevin, *Material Dreams: Southern California through the 1920s,* Oxford University Press, 1990.

37. Starr, Kevin, *Endangered Dreams: The Great Depression in California,* Oxford University Press, 1996.

38. Stevens, Errol Wayne, *Radical L.A.: From Coxey's Army to the Watts Riots, 1894-1965,* University of Oklahoma Press, Norman, 2009.

39. Stevenson, David, *With Our Backs to the Wall: Victory and Defeat in 1918,* Penguin Books, 2011.

40. Stimson, Grace H., *Rise of the Labor Movement in Los Angeles,* 1955, University of California Press.

41. Surface, Frank M. and Raymond L. Bland, *American Food in World War and Reconstruction Period: Operations in the Organizations under the Direction of Herbert Hoover 1914-1924,* Stanford University Press, 1931.

42. Susman, Warren, *Culture as History: The Transformation of American Society in the Twentieth Century,* Pantheon Books, New York, 1973.

43. Tygiel, Jules, *the Great Los Angeles Swindle: Oil, Stocks, and Scandal during the Roaring Twenties,* University of California Press, 1994.

44. Tuchman, Barbara W, *the Guns of August,* Ballantine Books *New York, 1962.*

Journals and Periodicals

1. D.J. Alexander, "Ecological Aspects of Influenza A Viruses in Animals and Their Relationship to Human Influenza: A Review," Journal of the Royal Society of Medicine 75 (October 1982): 799–811.

2. American Relief Administration Bulletin No. 1: Its origin, organization, program and international connections with documents in full, 17 March 1919.

3. John M. Barry, "The site of origin of the 1918 influenza pandemic and its public health implications," Journal of Translational Medicine, 20 (January 2004), 2-3.

4. John M. Barry, "Journal of the Plague Year, 1918 Outbreak", Smithsonian (November 1917): 34-43,

5. G.G. Brownlee, G.G., and E. Fodor, "the predicted antigenicity of the haemagglutinin of the 1918 Spanish influenza pandemic suggests an avian origin", Phil. Trans. Soc. Lond. 356 (2001):1871-1876.

6. E. Fodor, Louise Devenish, Othmar G. Engelhardt, Peter Palese, George G. Brownlee, and Adolfo Garcia-Sastre, "Rescue of Influenza a Virus from Recombinant DNA", Journal of Virology *Vol 73 no.11 (Nov. 1999): 9679-9682.*

7. William B. Friedricks, "Capital and Labor in Los Angeles: Henry E. Huntington vs. Organized Labor 1900-1920", Pacific Historical Review 59 No.3 (1990), 375-395.

8. Malcolm Gladwell, *"The Dead Zone,"* the New Yorker-Archive/ Reporter-at-Large, (Sept. 29, 1997).

9. Alan J. Hay, Victoria Gregory, Alan R. Douglas and Yi Pu Lin, "The evolution of human influenza viruses", Phil. Trans. R. Soc. Lond. B 356 (2001), 1861-1870.

10. Claude Hannoun, "Spanish Influenza in France: 1918-19", Hist. Sci. Med. 38 no.2 (Apr-June 2004), 165-175.

11. Nathan Lewis, "Was the Gold Standard the Cause of the Great Depression?" Forbes Magazine, Apr 1, 2012.

12. Melinda Liu, "Animal Vector, the Birth of a Killer," Smithsonian (November 2017), 44-51.

13. Maryn McKenna, "How to Stop a Lethal Virus," Smithsonian (November 2017) 52-61.

14. J. Oxford, "The so-called Great Spanish Influenza Pandemic of 1918 may have originated in France in 1916," Phil. Trans. R. Soc. Lond. B, 256 (2001), 1857-1859.

15. David K. Randall, "The Making of Malibu: How Malibu went from private paradise to Hollywood enclave," Lapham's Quarterly, (March 10, 2016), 1-9.

16. Ann Reid, Thomas G. Fanning, Johan V. Hultin, and Jeffery K. Taubenberger, "Origin and evolution of the 1918 "Spanish" Influenza virus hemagglutinin gene", Proc. Natl. Acad. Sci. USA Vol 96 (February 1999), 1651-1656.

17. Ann Reid, Thomas G. Fanning, Thomas A. Janczewski, and Jeffery K. Taubenberger, "Characterization of the 1918 "Spanish" Influenza virus neuraminidase gene," Proc. Natl. Acad. Sci. USA, Vol 97,6785-6790.

18. W.W. Robinson, "The Southern California Real Estate Boom of the Twenties," The Quarterly Historical Society of Southern California, Vol. 24 no.1 (March 1942), 25-30.

19. Robert Speers, "Harold Ferguson's Own Story," Los Angeles Record, (February 11, 1931).

20. N. Sriwilaijaroen, and Yasuo Suzuki, "Molecular basis of the structure and function of H1 hemagglutinin of influenza virus," Proc. Jpn. Acad., Ser. B 88 (2012), 226-249.

21. Jeffrey K. Taubenberger, Ann H. Reid, Thomas A. Janczewski and Thomas G. Fanning, "Integrating historical, clinical and molecular genetic data in order to explain the origin and virulence of the 1918 Spanish influenza virus," Phil. Trans. R. Soc. London B 356 (2001), 1829-1839.

22. Jeffrey K. Taubenberger," Influenza: Trying to Catch a Moving Target". Scientific American, (November 11, *2013).*

23. Jeffrey K. Taubenberger, Ann H. Reid, Thomas G. Fanning, "Capturing a Killer Flu Virus". Scientific American, (April 27, 2009).

24. Dan Vergano, "1918 Flu Pandemic That Killed 50 Million Originated in China, Historians Say", National Geographic Magazine (January 24, 2014).

25. RG Webster, WJ Bean, OT Gorman, TM Chambers, "Evolution and Ecology of Influenza A Viruses". Microbiological Reviews 56 no.1 (March 1992): 152-179.

Index

A

AEF (American Expeditionary Force), xiii–xiv, 5, 8–9, 11–13, 24, 27–28, 31–32, 60, 84–85, 119, 209
AFIP (Armed Forces Institute of Pathology), 37, 41–42
AFL (American Federation of Labor), 100, 102, 117
Allies, 12–14, 32, 59, 64–65, 67–69, 115, 204
Americanism, 83, 87–88, 106, 114
American Legion, 83, 85–90, 105–7, 116–17, 145, 221
American Legion Weekly, 86, 88
ARA (American Relief Administration), 1, 60, 69–72, 151, 197
armistice, xiv–xv, 1, 36, 38, 53–56, 69, 83, 86, 106, 132, 198
ARU (American Railway Union), 78
Asquith, Herbert, 62–63

B

BAF (Better America Federation), 99, 104
Bell, J. Franklin, 26
Belleau Wood, 14, 33
Beverly Crest Syndicate, 168
Boulder Dam, 168–69
Brady, T. C., 161
British blockade, 61, 63, 69
Burroughs, Edgar Rice, 174

C

California Criminal Syndicalism Act, 102
California National Guard, 3–4
California Trust Company, 159
Canoga Estates, 161–62, 177
Central Powers, xiv, 4, 13–14, 115
chamber of commerce, 97, 99, 103, 107, 139, 164, 200
Chandler, Harry, 103–4, 130–32, 136, 140, 143, 145, 160
Churchill, Winston, 62
Clemenceau, Georges, 69
Clinton, Clifford, ix, xv
Committee for Public Information, 9, 64
Communist Party, 117
communists, 101, 104, 114, 117
Congress, 70, 148, 169, 172, 198–99, 205, 207–9
CRB (Commission for Relief in Belgium), 61–63
Creel, George, 9, 64

D

Debs, Eugene, 78–79, 113
DeMille, Cecille B., 142
Dot. *See* Gordon, Dolores
Downs, James, 37, 41

E

Edison Trust, 142
Evans-Ferguson Company, 159
Everest, Wesley, 107

F

FA (Field Artillery), 3, 5, 21, 24–25, 30, 47, 127
famine, mass, 61, 68–69
Federal Aid Highway Act, 172
Federal Reserve System, 199, 201–2, 207
Ferguson, Alexander, 130, 229
Ferguson, Harold Gale, xiii, 1–2, 5, 29, 51, 79, 88, 93, 100, 130, 132–33, 144, 159, 166–67, 183
  arraignment of, 184
  diary of, ix, xv, 80
  in France, 21
  incarceration of, 221
  introduction to unionism, 105
  as manager for Lake Arrowhead, 163
  pardon of, 192
  training in San Diego, 14
  verdict of, 189
Ferguson, Lillian Prest, 2, 55, 73, 130, 132
Ferguson, Peter, 2, 15, 130, 132–33
Ferguson, Vernon, ix
Flint, Motley, 184
flu. *See* influenza
food relief, xv, 53–54, 59–60, 62–63, 69, 197

G

GAR (Grand Army of the Republic), 84
George, David Lloyd, 12
Gilmore, Earl, 168
Goodyear, Anson C., 71
Gordon, Dolores, 73, 132–33, 221

Great Depression, 180, 189, 202–3, 205, 207
Great War, xv, 179
Gregory, Tom, 54, 57–58
Grey, Edward, 62
Griffith, D. W., 142
Grimm, Warren, 108

H

Haight, Raymond I., 182–83, 185–86
Haldeman, Harry E., 104
Hammond, William, 37
Harold G. Ferguson Corporation, 159–62, 164–66, 168, 173, 175–76, 180–81, 183–84, 211, 214
Haywood, William D. "Big Bill," 101
H. G. Ferguson Building Corporation, 183
Hollywood Post American Legion, 80, 89
Hoover, Herbert, xiv–xv, 1, 54, 60–72, 169, 179, 197–200, 202, 204, 206–9, 221
Huntington, Henry, 76–78, 117, 131

I

Imperial Valley, 2, 169
influenza, 11, 30–31, 33–39, 42–43, 56
  epidemic, 34–35
  pandemic, 11, 14, 29, 35–36, 72
  Spanish, 1, 30–31, 39, 41, 231
ITU (International Typographical Union), 96, 98
IWW (International Workers of the World), 78, 83, 90, 100–102, 104–9, 113
IWW members, 104, 106, 108

J

Jazz Singer, The, 143–44
Jewish Welfare Board, 24, 27–28
Jolson, Al, 143–44, 168

K

Kellogg, Vernon, 62, 69
Knights of Columbus, 24–25,
    27–28

L

labor, 56, 60, 78, 98, 100, 102,
    113, 142
  organized, 95, 99, 112–13
labor movement, 93, 96, 101
Labor Movement, The
    (Tannenbaum), 113
labor strikes, 71, 94–95
Lake Arrowhead, 163–64, 177
Lake Arrowhead Company, 163
Lankershim, Isaac, 135
Lankershim, James Boone, 135
LATU (Los Angeles Typographical
    Union), 97–98
Los Angeles Pacific Boulevard and
    Development Company, 131
Los Angeles Times, x, 78, 96–97,
    140, 145
Luckey, Clayton, 166, 184–88, 190

M

MacMillan, Margaret, 53–54, 227
Malibu Syndicate, 177, 185–
    86, 190
March, Peyton C., 13
McDowell, Jack, 74, 89–90, 105,
    133, 143
McNamara, James, 98, 226
McNamara, John, 98

Merriam, Frank, 192
Meuse-Argonne, 14, 33, 35
M&M (Merchants and
    Manufacturers' Association),
    102–3

N

Nationalists, 111
NWLB (National War Labor
    Board), 79

O

open-shop policy, 76–77, 97
Orchards, Earl, 166–67
Otis, Harrison Gray, 96–98, 102
Owens Valley Water, 136, 169

P

Pacific Electric, 75–77, 99, 136
Pacific National Bank, 165–
    66, 177
pandemic, 32–33, 36, 38, 40,
    42–43
Pershing, John J., xiv, 11–12, 27,
    34, 119
Pickford, Mary, 142, 174
pneumonia, secondary, 33–35
Progressivism, 111–12
Pullman, George, 78

R

RFC (Reconstruction Finance
    Corporation), 208
Rindge, Frederick, 170–71
Rindge, May, 170–72, 175
Roosevelt, Theodore, 8, 10, 12
Roosevelt, Theodore, Jr., 85
Russian Revolution, 65, 114–
    15, 117

S

Selective Service System, 10
Sherman, Moses, 130, 136, 160
Shope, Richard, 38–39
Smoot-Hawley Tariff, 205
socialism, 111–14
Socialist Party, 79, 101–2, 112–14, 117
socialists, 78, 104, 112, 114–15
Somme Offensive, 14, 35
Southern California, 77, 93, 95, 117, 129, 139, 142, 146–47, 149, 170–71, 181
Southern Pacific railroad, 73, 75, 78, 95, 112, 171
Stephens, William, 102
stock market crash, 179–80, 204
Supreme Economic Council, 69

T

talkies, 143–44
Tannenbaum, Frank, 113
  The Labor Movement
Taubenberger, Jeffrey, 39, 41–42
Taylor, Alonzo, 69
Times bombing, 98–99, 112
Treaty of Versailles, 54, 203
trusts, 7, 142, 159–60, 165–66, 175–77, 181–83, 185–91
  private, 166, 176, 183

U

union, 76–79, 81, 97, 100–102, 106, 109, 117, 222
unionism, radical, 103, 105
University Club of Los Angeles, 164
US Food Administration, 60, 63–67, 154

V

Van Nuys, 135–36, 164
Vaughn, Roscoe, 36–37, 41
Vienna, 54, 57, 68–69, 203
virus
  influenza, 38–40, 42
  swine, 39

W

Walsh, Raoul, 174
War Department, 27, 66–67
W.B. Causey, 58
Wilson, Woodrow, xiii, xv, 3, 8–11, 59, 63–64, 66, 68–71, 115
Wobblies, 101, 103, 105–7, 109
World Series, 79–80
World War I, ix, xi, xiii–xiv, 1, 21–22, 60, 76, 84, 93, 129, 141, 180, 204, 221
World War II, xv, 1